CW00450053

Sea View
Camping

V̌icarious
Books LLP

Special thanks to: Susan Glossop, Gill Sadler, Dave Brodley, Grenville Weston, Russ and Mandy Valentine, Michelle Allen, Janice Sadler.

First published in Great Britain by Brian M. Leahy, 2006.

Reprinted 2007. This edition published 2008.

© Vicarious Books LLP 2007, 2008.

Copyright © text Vicarious Books LLP. All rights reserved.

Copyright © photographs Vicarious Books LLP unless otherwise stated.

ISBN: 978-0-9552808-3-2

Compiling GPS co-ordinates into a list contravenes copyright law.

Vicarious Books LLP, 62 Tontine Street, Folkestone, Kent, CT20 1JP. Tel: 0131 2083333
www.vicariousbooks.co.uk

Editors: Meli George and Chris Doree

Design and artwork by: Chris Gladman Design Tel: 07745 856652

Front cover
Main picture: View from Beachside Holiday Park.
Small pictures: Trewethett Farm, Sandaway Beach Holiday Park, Damage Barton.

Back cover
Main picture: Land's End
Small Pictures: Beach near Trewince Farm, Nicholaston Farm Caravan Site.

Welcome to Sea View Camping

Truly breathtaking sea views really make exhilarating starts to your day. As your breakfast sizzles on the stove, you hear the waves crashing on the beach, the rising sun warms the dew in the grass and you sit back and wonder why you ever went to work. If that sounds appealing then you picked up the right book.

This unique guide shows you all the sea view campsites around Great Britain. All you have to do is choose where you want to go and be ready for a fantastic time as you explore one of the most diverse coastlines in the world. There are campsites perched on the edge of fantastic Jurassic cliff tops, some right on deserted sandy beaches surrounded by hundreds of acres of dunes and others with every convenience a family could desire. If you love being by the sea then this is the guide for you.

Because everybody has different requirements all the sea view campsites and parks around mainland Great Britain have been listed in this guide. Whether they are small five pitch sites, 28 day camping fields or large holiday parks and everything in between they're in the guide. That way you can choose the right site for you.

To help you make informed choices, a photo of the sea view from each inspected site is included. Descriptions are given about the sites, their facilities and amenities, especially if beach access is possible. In addition the location of the nearest pub, shop, beach and slipway is provided to further enhance your choice.

Putsborough Sands, Devon

Sand Castles at Sunrise

Welsh Coastal Path

Traeth
Porth Neigwl
(Treheli)
Beach

Gallwch ddilyn Llwybr
Arfordir Llŷn drwy gerdded
ar hyd y traeth hwn.

You can follow the
Llŷn Coastal Path by walking
along this beach.

Gofal	Caution
Byddwch yn wyliadwrus o'r llanw.	Be aware of tidal conditions.
Peidiwch â dringo creigiau na chlogwyni.	Do not climb rocks or cliffs.
Cymerwch ofal arbennig yn ystod tywydd stormus.	Take extra care during stormy weather.

View from Lizard Peninsula, Cornwall

4

CONTENTS

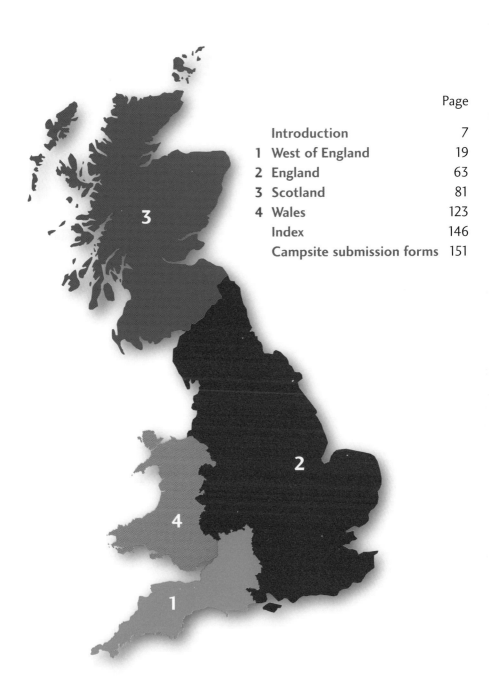

Mussels and Mushrooms

Lifebuoy, Somerset

Cornish Fishing Harbour

Origins of this guide

Brian M Leahy first published Sea View Camping in 2004. Like you, he wanted to see the sea when he was camping. Because he couldn't find a suitable campsite guide he decided to travel around the coast of Great Britain and write one himself. For the second edition Brian selected his favourite 150 sites and produced a full colour guide with photographs. In 2007 Vicarious Books took over the title and developed it into what you are reading today. Brian's favourite 150 sites were re-inspected and make up most of the featured campsites in this guide, a further 100 campsites are listed at the back of the four regions of this book. Undoubtedly many of the campsites that are text only listings do indeed have excellent sea views and facilities. This will provide something to discover for the more adventurous, but please remember to take photos and fill in the submissions forms at the rear of this guide.

Campsite selection and inspection

Every campsite with a known sea view has been included in this guide. Campsites are listed on this basis alone, so big or small, if the sea can be seen that's it. Campsites cannot pay to be included or become a featured site in the guide, nor do we take their word for it, but inspect the sites to check the view, facilities and amenities. The quality or quantity of facilities and amenities are not formally judged, but are listed with comments for your convenience.

Consistency of inspections.

Our inspectors are some of the most experienced and knowledgeable campers in the country, they all regularly travel in the UK and Europe. Their expertise has been used to evaluate the campsites. Inspections were carried out in August, when campsites are at their busiest and under the most pressure. Only three inspectors were commissioned each having specific geographical areas.

Inspector profile

Don & Maureen Madge: Never at home for long, Don and Maureen regularly travel the length and breadth of Europe. They toured Scotland for the fourth time to inspect sites for Sea View Camping, they also inspected sites in mainland England.

Andy & Nette Clarke: When not out and about Andy is busy with his excellent website www.ukmotorhomes.net Sea View Camping had them touring Wales and inspecting sites.

Chris Doree & Meli George: The editors of this guide are regular travellers in Europe when not behind their desks at Vicarious Books Folkestone HQ. They travelled around the West Country inspecting sites.

Vicarious Books LLP

Vicarious Books specialises in motorhome and camping books, both publishing and importing unique guides. For a list of guides available from Vicarious Books, see the inside front cover of this guide or visit www.VicariousBooks.co.uk

Scottish Ruins

Land's End, Cornwall

Wheal Coates Tin Mine, St Agnes, Cornwall

Nicholaston Farm Caravan and Camping Site, Penmaen, Swansea

Freshly caught seafood supper

Open Air Theatre, Folkestone, Kent

THE LIZARD POINT
GIFT SHOP

Fishing in Kent

HOW TO USE THIS GUIDE

Campsite locator - This guide is split into four colour coded geographical regions, West of England, England, Scotland and Wales. Overview maps are located at the beginning of each region, numbers printed on the maps identify and show the location of each campsite. On the opposite page of each regional map the name of each campsite is given against the corresponding map reference number. Campsites are listed alphabetically by name within each region, for cross-reference the corresponding map reference number is printed beside the campsite name.

Entry explanation

1   Campsite name

2   Campsite map reference number

3   Campsite address and phone number

4   Campsite website – where available

5   Photo from campsite of sea view

6   Units accepted by campsite

   Å   *Tent*

      Touring caravan

      Motorhome

      Large vehicles - Motorhome/Caravan/5th Wheel. Campsites were checked for suitability and the owners/managers were asked whether very large vehicles were accommodated onsite. Access should be possible by a competent experienced driver. Most campsites only accept very large vehicles with advanced bookings and we insist that you discuss access and pitch availability with campsite staff before arrival.

      Holiday accommodation for hire – Many of the campsites in this guide have other accommodation for hire, for example static caravans, holiday homes, chalets or lodges. This accommodation has not been inspected and may have a better or worse sea view than described.

7   **Description** – An unbiased description is given about the site and the sea view. The strengths or weaknesses and appeal of the site are provided. Further useful information is also given.

8   **Symbols** – The following symbols are used to identify the size and facilities of the site. All sites have a water tap and a toilet disposal point unless otherwise stated. Facility only available when highlighted.

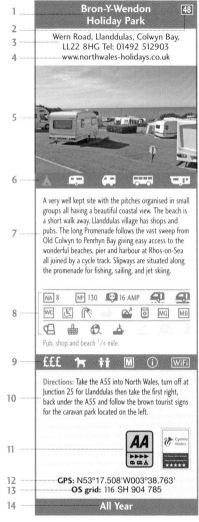

1	**Bron-Y-Wendon** 48 **Holiday Park**
2	
3	Wern Road, Llanddulas, Colwyn Bay, LL22 8HG Tel: 01492 512903
4	www.northwales-holidays.co.uk

5

6   Å

7   A very well kept site with the pitches organised in small groups all having a beautiful coastal view. The beach is a short walk away. Llanddulas village has shops and pubs. The long Promenade follows the vast sweep from Old Colwyn to Penrhyn Bay giving easy access to the wonderful beaches, pier and harbour at Rhos-on-Sea all joined by a cycle track. Slipways are situated along the promenade for fishing, sailing, and jet skiing.

8   NA 8   NP 130   16 AMP

WC   MG   MB

Pub, shop and beach 1/4 mile.

9   £££   M   WiFi

10   Directions: Take the A55 into North Wales, turn off at Junction 25 for Llanddulas then take the first right, back under the A55 and follow the brown tourist signs for the caravan park located on the left.

11   AA ▶▶▶▶   Cymru Wales ★★★★★

12   **GPS:** N53°17.508'W003°38.763'
13   **OS grid:** 116 SH 904 785

14   **All Year**

NA	Number of acres where known
NP	Number of pitches
	Electricity available and amperage where known
	Level pitches
	All season/hard standing pitches
WC	Toilets
	Disabled toilets
	Showers
	Family bathroom
	Dishwashing facilities
	Laundry

MG Motorhome grey water disposal

MB Motorhome toilet waste disposal

The following symbols identify that the amenities are either onsite or within five minutes walk unless otherwise indicated. The facilities have not been tested and charges may apply.

Pub/bar

Shop

Beach

Slipway

Swimming pool indoor or outdoor

Children's play area

Footpath

9 Information Symbols

Cost – The cost of the campsite is indicated by the £ symbols. All prices are based on two people, one caravan or motorhome with electric in August. Prices are offered as a guideline only and should always be confirmed in advance.

£ Up to £10 per night

££ £10-17 per night

£££ £17-35 per night

££££ £35 plus per night

Many campsites allow dogs onsite, this is indicated by the dog symbol. Confirmation must always be sought in advance that your dog(s) can be accommodated. Many campsites charge extra for dogs. There may be a limit on the number of dogs allowed on site and some sites specify the type of units that dogs can be accommodated with. Some breeds are disallowed on some sites, always check your breed is permitted before arrival. Campsite owners and other holidaymakers expect dogs to be kept quiet and under control at all times and usually on a lead. Dogs must be exercised in appropriate areas or offsite and all mess to be cleared in a responsible fashion. In addition it is advised that you never leave your dog unattended.

This symbol refers to adults only campsites. No person under the age of 18 will be admitted.

M This symbol refers to member only campsites. Generally these belong to either the Camping and Caravanning Club or the Caravan Club and a valid membership is required to stay, though it may be possible to join at reception. The name of the club is usually indicated in the title of the campsite. CS and CL sites are also for members only.

CS *(Certified Sites)* - Camping and Caravanning Club members' only, small sites restricted to five caravans or motorhomes, plus tents, space permitting.

CL *(Certified Locations)* - Caravan Club members' only, small sites restricted to five caravans or motorhomes.

Internet available (charges may apply).

WiFi WiFi available (charges may apply).

10 **Directions** – Directions are provided. Please note that many campsites near the sea are down narrow lanes with passing places.

11 **Awards** – Awards by the tourist board and the AA are indicted here. See page 12 for more information on the award systems.

12 **OS grid references** – These refer to the Ordinance Survey Landranger 1:50,000 maps. The first three numbers and the two letters refers to the map identification code, the remaining numbers create a six-figure grid reference.

13 **GPS Co-ordinates** – These are presented in the N53°17.508'W003°38.763' format and were taken at the site entrance. Please note that directions should always be checked when using a satellite navigation machines, as they may not select the best route for your unit. Postcodes do not always provide accurate destinations when used with satellite navigators.

14 **Opening dates** – Opening dates change year to year and are given as an indication only, please check with the campsite before arrival.

Text only listings – At the end of each chapter there are text only listing for sites that have not been inspected since 2004. The name, address, phone number, web address and directions are included. It is believed that all these sites had a sea view in 2004, however things change and campers are advised to check with the campsite before arrival to avoid disappointment.

HOW TO USE THIS GUIDE

Awards

Visit Britain and the AA inspect holiday, touring and camping parks around Britain.

Visit Britain – The Visit Britain team of professional assessors visit each park every year. They spend time at the park checking all the facilities and award a quality score for every aspect. Parks don't miss out on stars by not having certain facilities but what they do offer customers must be of the very highest standard in order to receive the top ratings.

All holiday parks with these star ratings will meet the minimum standards, which include, among other things: Meet all statutory obligations including site licence, public liability and fire and safety requirements. Meet minimum quality standards of maintenance and cleanliness as set out by tourism assessing bodies. Provide toilet and washing facilities with hot and cold running water.

Visit Britain rates caravan and camping sites and parks from one to five stars. More stars indicate a greater level of facilities or quality.

★   Simple, practical, no frills

★★   Well presented and well run

★★★   Good level of quality and comfort

★★★★   Excellent standard throughout

★★★★★ Exceptional with a degree of luxury

The AA Pennant scheme – The AA's Pennant rating scheme has a five-point scale based on the site's style and the range of facilities. As the Pennant rating increases, so the quality and variety of facilities and amenities is greater. The AA Pennant rating is only based on the touring pitches and the facilities at campsites and caravan parks. AA inspectors do not visit or report on rented static caravans or chalets.

►   A simple standard of facilities.

►►   A better level of facilities, services, customer care and maintenance.

►►►   A very good standard with well maintained facilities and grounds..

►►►►   An extremely high standard in all areas.

►►►►►   An extremely high standard. Facilities, security and customer care are exceptional.

Bay View Farm, Cornwall. *Photo campsite owner.*

Folkestone Harbour, Kent

Perran Sands, Cornwall

Burnham-on-Sea, Somerset

Gower, West Glamorgan

Ardmair Point, Ross-shire

Durdle Door, Dorset

Looe Harbour, Cornwall

Life Boat at Land's End, Cornwall

Lyme Regis, Dorset

Heather on Exmoor, Devon

Sunset from North Hill, Somerset

Zigzag Path, Folkestone Coastal Park, Kent

Footpath to Land's End, Cornwall

Crail Harbour, near Sauchope Links Caravan Park, Fife © Keith & Natalie Williams

Fishing at Branscombe, Devon

© Alf Alderson www.alfalderson.co.uk

Coastal footpath to Watchet, Somerset

Lizard Peninsula, Cornwall

Woolacombe Bay, Devon

The Lost Gardens of Heligan, Cornwall

ENGLAND THE WEST

Cornish Harbour

Trawlers

St Michael's Mount, Cornwall

Wheal Coates Tin Mine, St Agnes, Cornwall
Near Beacon Cottage Farm Campsite

The Eden Project, Cornwall

Blackpool Sands, Devon

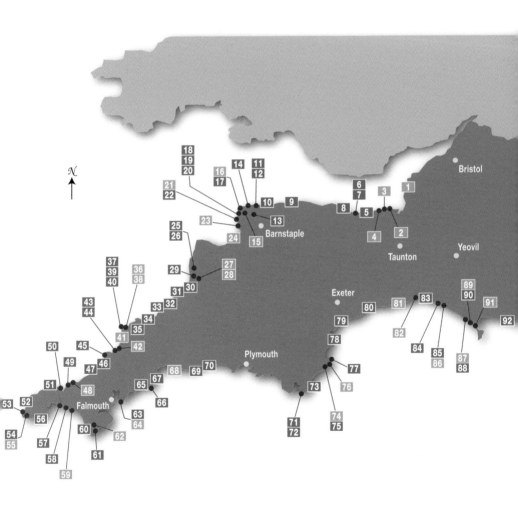

Map	Campsite	Page	Map	Campsite	Page
1	Slimeridge Farm Touring Park	62	48	St Ives Bay Holiday Park	62
2	Staple Farm CL	48	49	Beachside Holiday Park	26
3	Home Farm Holiday Centre	61	50	Ayr Holiday Park	24
4	St Audries Bay Holiday Club	62	51	Trevalgan Touring Park	51
5	Helwell Bay Holidays	33	52	Trevedra Farm Caravan and Camping Site	53
6	Warren Bay Holiday Village	56	53	Higher Tregiffian Farm	61
7	Warren Farm	57	54	Sennen Cove Camping and Caravan Park	46
8	Minehead Camping and Caravanning Club Site	38	55	Brea Vean Farm	60
9	Caffyns Farm	27	56	Kemyel Crease CL	36
10	Napps Touring Holidays	40	57	Kenneggy Cove Holiday Park	36
11	Damage Barton	30	58	Higher Pentreath Farm	34
12	Sandaway Beach Holiday Park	44	59	Bosverbas	60
13	Sunnymead Farm	49	60	Teneriffe Farm	49
14	Easewell Farm Holiday Park	31	61	Chycarne Holiday Park	28
15	Mullacott Farm	61	62	Gwendreath Farm Caravan Park	60
16	Woolacombe Sands Holiday Park	62	63	Trewince Farm	55
17	North Morte Farm	41	64	Arthurs Field	60
18	Europa Park	32	65	Seaview International Holiday Park	46
19	Warcombe Farm Camping Park	56	66	Treveague Farm Campsite	52
20	Woolacombe Bay Holiday Village	59	67	Pentewan Sands Holiday Park	43
21	Mitchums & Myrtle Campsite	61	68	Penhale Caravan & Camping Park	61
22	Putsborough Sands	42	69	West Wayland Touring Park	57
23	Deer Park Holiday Estate	60	70	Bay View Farm Camping and Caravan Site	25
24	Braddicks Holiday Centre	60	71	Mollie Tuckers Field CL	39
25	Ivyleaf CL	35	72	Stephens Field	48
26	Penhalt Farm Holiday Park	42	73	Slapton Sands Camping and Caravanning Site	47
27	Wooda Farm Park	62	74	Twitchen Parc	62
28	Penstowe Caravan & Camping Park	61	75	Hillhead Caravan Club Site	35
29	Sandymouth Bay Holiday Park	45	76	Leonards Cove	61
30	Bude Camping and Caravanning Club Site	60	77	Beverley Park Caravan & Camping Site	27
31	Widemouth Bay Caravan Park	58	78	Coast View	29
32	Trewethett Farm Caravan Club Site	54	79	Ladram Bay Caravan Site	37
33	The Headland Caravan Park	50	80	Salcombe Regis Camping and Caravan Park	44
34	Lower Pennycrocker Farm	38	81	Manor Farm Caravan Site	61
35	Chapel Farm CL	28	82	Seadown Holiday Park	61
36	Higher Harlyn Park	60	83	Golden Cap	33
37	Mothers Ivey's Bay	39	84	Highland End Holiday Park	34
38	Atlantic View	60	85	Eype House Caravan Park	31
39	Trethias Farm Caravan Park	51	86	West Bay Holiday Park	62
40	Treyamon Bay	55	87	Bagwell Farm Touring Park	60
41	Trevornick Holiday Park	62	88	Windridge CL	58
42	Watergate Bay Touring Park	62	89	Littlesea Holiday Park	61
43	Tregurrian Camping and Caravanning Club Site	50	90	Pebble Bank	40
44	Trevean Caravan & Camping Park	52	91	East Fleet Farm Touring Park	60
45	Beacon Cottage Farm	26	92	Durdle Door Holiday Park	30
46	Trevellas Manor farm	53			
47	St. Agnes Beacon Caravan Club Site	47			

Ayr Holiday Park
50

St Ives, Cornwall, TR26 1EJ
Tel: 01736 795855   www.ayrholidaypark.co.uk

This campsite is conveniently located in the suburbs high above St Ives. The campsites' elevated position enables excellent views across St Ives bay, which can be enjoyed from most touring pitches and static caravans. During the day you can watch the surfers and swimmers, at night the illuminations set the scene. St Ives harbour is a half a mile downhill walk; thankfully you can catch a bus back. The campsite facilities are exceptionally good. Unsurprisingly this is a popular site. There are local shops and pubs close by.

Directions: Follow A30 past Hayle, then take St Ives exit. 300 yards after leaving the A30, turn left at the second mini roundabout following directions to St Ives for heavy vehicles. After a couple of miles join the B3306 and turn right for St Ives. Turn left at a mini roundabout signposted 'Ayr and Porthmeor beach'. Follow the road through a housing estate and you will reach the park entrance after a sharp 'S' bend.

| NA | 10 | NP | 68 | 16 AMP | | |

| WC | | | | | | MG |

GPS: N50°12.752'W005°29.372'
OS grid: 203 SW 511 405

Pub, shop, beach and slipway at St Ives.

All Year

Bay View Farm Camping and Caravan Site 70

St Martins, Looe, Cornwall, PL13 1NZ
Tel: 01503 265922/07967 267312 www.looebaycaravans.co.uk

££

WiFi

Two things make this site exceptional. The view is captivating, looking over Looe bay from an elevated position you watch the daily comings and goings of fishing boats, at night the town lights reflect in the water. Second Mike the owner has a friendly, laid-back approach, which creates a very special atmosphere. Mike's friendly shire horses graze adjacent paddocks. From site you can walk down to the beach, but it is uphill all the way back, or to Looe on the coast path. Famous for its same day caught, daily fish market, Looe is a pretty seaside town with pubs, restaurants and a sandy beach. Fishermen love it here as many charter boats offer everything from Mackerel to Shark Fishing trips.

Directions: Leave A38 at Trerulefoot seven miles West of Plymouth, take A374 for one mile. Turn right onto the A387 towards Looe. At Widegates take the B3253 to Looe then turn left after one mile at No Mans Land. Follow signs to the Monkey Sanctuary. At the entrance to the Monkey Sanctuary bear right. Half a mile down a cul-de-sac the site is on the right at the end of the lane.

NA 5   NP 20   16 AMP

WC

Pub, shop, beach and slipway at Looe.

GPS: N50°21.839'W004°25.777'
OS grid: 201 SX 274 545

All Year

Beachside Holiday Park `49`

Hayle, Cornwall, TR27 5AW
Tel: 01736 753080
www.beachside.co.uk

Nestled amongst hundreds of acres of sand dunes this unique campsite occupies 20 acres. Some pitching areas are gently sloping and all are spread through an amazing complex of sand dunes that any child would love to play within. Not all the pitches have views but from some you can see the sea stretching to St Ives. There is plenty to explore and there is direct access to an enormous quiet sandy beach via a walkway leading through the dunes. Closest to the sea there is a small complex of retro holiday chalets for hire.

| NA | 20 | NP | 80 | 10 AMP | | |

£££

Directions: Leave the A30 into the Hayle exit at the large roundabout and take the Hayle road. Turn right by the putting green and follow the brown tourist signs to site.

GPS: N50°12.132'W005°24.903'
OS grid: 203 SW 564 389

Easter - September

Beacon Cottage Farm Touring Park `45`

Beacon Drive, St. Agnes, Cornwall
TR5 0NU Tel: 01872 552347
www.beaconcottagefarmholidays.co.uk

© Jane Sawle

As you enter the site you are greeted by beautifully kept stone farm buildings, now used by the campsite, that makes up part of this traditional working Cornish family farm. There are some very secluded and cosy pitching spots but the two main camping fields give excellent tranquil cliff and sea views as far as St Ives. This is a family friendly site on the South West Coastal path with the captivating remains of Wheal Coates tin mine is just 200 metres away.

| NA | 4 | NP | 60 | 10 AMP | | |

Pub and shop 2 miles at St Agnes.

£££

Directions: From the A30 turn right at Chiverton roundabout onto B3277 signposted St. Agnes. In three miles past Presingall Barns turn left at the mini roundabout signposted Chapel Porth. At the next mini roundabout in approximately four miles turn left. Here you will see a brown tourism sign to Beacon Cottage Farm and you follow these signs to the park which is approximately 1 1/2 miles. Narrow with passing places at times. Walkers welcome.

GPS: N50°18.339'W005°13.515'
OS grid: 203 SW 703 501

April - October

Beverley Park Caravan & Camping Site [77]

Goodrington Road, Paignton, Devon,
TQ4 7JE Tel: 01803 843887
www.beverley-holidays.co.uk

This is a family orientated holiday complex with lots and lots of excellent facilities. There are plenty of static caravans for hire and two main camping fields but the pitches with best sea view are on a mostly sloping area. The Top Bar has an outside terrace overlooking the large heated outdoor pool, camping fields onto the sea and English Riviera. Everywhere is very well kept, clean and tidy.

| NA 20 | NP 180 | 16 AMP | | |

Directions: Turn off into Goodrington Road signposted 'Methodist church'. Follow road up hill and Beverley Park signposted on left.

GPS: N50°24.828'W003°34.117'
OS grid: 202 SX 886 582

All Year

Caffyns Farm CL [9]

Lynton, Devon EX35 6JW
Tel: 01598 753524
www.caravanclub.co.uk

This is a simple five pitch grass paddock CL, about 1 1/2 acres in size, on a traditional livestock farm. Occupying an elevated position the sea can be seen from anywhere you chose to pitch, this is a place to escape from it all. The charming owner was born and bred here and has run the CL for many years. The Lynton to Barnstable steam railways' Woody Bay Station is one mile away.

| NA 1 1/2 | NP 5 | | |

Pub and shop 1 1/2 miles. Slipway at Lynmouth.

Directions: A361. Turn right off the A36 Tiverton to Barnstaple road at the roundabout onto the A399 road signposted Combe Martin and Blackmoor Gate. In 11 3/4 miles at Blackmoor Gate turn right onto the A39 road signposted Lynton and Lynmouth. In 5 1/2 miles at Caffyns cross roads turn left signposted Caffyns and in 50 yards keep left and in half a mile turn right into the farm road. The site entrance is on the left in 350 yards.

GPS: N51°12.992'W003°52.422'
OS grid: 180 SS 691 481

May - September

Chapel Farm CL **[35]**

Edmonton, Wadebridge, Cornwall, PL27 7JA
Tel: 01208 812011
www.caravanclub.co.uk

Tucked away in a rural location this informal five pitch site is level at top then slopes away. All pitches give countryside views then the estuary, out to sea and Padstow. Visitors are trusted to pay in an honesty box. The local, very attractive country pub with an excellent reputation for food is only two minutes walk away.

| NA | 1 | NP | 5 | |

Pub 100 metres and shop on A39.

£££

Directions: On the A39 towards Truro turn off A39 on the right signposted 'Edmonton' just past Tesco (the nearest shop). Follow lane past the Quarryman pub on the right. When the road divides enter the site through the gate that divides both lanes.

GPS: N50°31.131'W004°52.468'
OS grid: 200 SW 963 728

April - October

Chycarne Holiday Park **[61]**

Kuggar, Ruan Minor, Helston, Cornwall,
TR12 7LX Tel: 01326 290200
www.camping-cornwall.com

A mix of chalets, mobile homes and camping facilities set within a sheltered, tree-lined site combine to provide a safe, friendly and relaxing base from which to explore. This is a pleasant site with half the touring pitches having a view of the sea. The site is quiet, comfortable and friendly with great stargazing at night.

| NA | 8 | NP | 100 | 16 AMP | |
| WC | | | | | |

Pub; Kennack Sands Inn. Beach 5 minutes.

£££

Directions: From A3083 towards lizard point turn left signposted 'Kenneck Sands'. Follow road and turn left for 'Kenneck Sands'. Follow road and site on left once you enter Kuggar.

GPS: N50°00.258'W005°10.575'
OS grid: 204 SW 725 164

April - October

Coast View 78

Torquay Road, Shaldon, Teignmouth, South Devon, TQ14 0BG
Tel: 01626 872392 www.coastview.co.uk

Many unfolding layers await you. This site is unique and the awesome panoramic sea view from top tent field is probably the widest in the country. You enter this steeply sloping site right in the heart of the busy entertainment area. As you climb the steep road you pass excellent chalets and static caravans onto the well laid out level touring pitches, past the camping terraces and on to the large informal camping fields where you should be able to pitch far from your neighbours and even further from the excellent facilities. This site has something, somewhere to suit everybody.

| NA 17 | NP 115 | 10 AMP | | |

| WC | | | | | |

Pub, shop and beach 1 mile at Shaldon.

Directions: Be aware of grounding on entering/exiting site. Adj to the A379 as exit Shaldon towards Torquay.

GPS: N50°32.104'W003°30.163'
OS grid: 203 SX 935 717

March - October

WEST OF ENGLAND

Damage Barton `11`

Mortehoe, Woolacombe, North Devon, EX34 7EJ Tel: 01271 870502
www.damagebarton.co.uk

A park of two halves. Being affiliated to both the caravan clubs this site maintains a high standard across the whole park. Just about every pitch has great sea views as far as the Welsh coast. Tractor tours of the 580 acre National Trust land, family run farm operate from May to September. Lee Bay is 1 1/2 miles about a 25 minute walk. Conveniently there is a bus stop at the campsite entrance.

| NA | 16 | | NP | 150 | | 10 AMP | |

Pub, shop at Morthoe. Beach at Woolacombe.

£££

Directions: From A361 through Barnstable and Braunton, turn left at Mullacott Cross roundabout on to the B3343 (signposted Mortehoe and Woolacombe). In approximately three miles turn right, signposted Mortehoe, the site entrance is on the right in one mile.

GPS: N51°11.025'W004°11.312'
OS grid: 180 SS 471 451

March - October

Durdle Door Holiday Park `92`

Lulworth Cove, Wareham, Dorset, BH20 5PU
Tel: 01929 400200
www.lulworth.com

© Helen Lethbridge

This is one of the few places on this section of coast where there is access to the sea, which many day visitors take advantage of. There are plenty of non-sea view pitches including a very pleasant area under pine trees ideal during hot spells. A single row set back from the cliff provides the few sea view pitches available. Most of these are so steep that only touring caravans can level and then require concrete blocks to perch on. Day parking spoils the tranquillity and attractive views.

| NA | 45 | | NP | 108 | | 16 AMP | |

Slipway 1 mile at Lulworth Cove.

£££

Directions: On the A31 past Ringwood to Bere Regis. From Bere Regis follow local signs to Wool, then take the B3071 to West Lulworth. Continue past The Castle Inn and the war memorial then taking the first right, continue past the church and up the hill, the entrance to Durdle Door Holiday Park is on the brow of the hill, on the left.

GPS: N50°37.612'W002°16.096'
OS grid: 194 SY 812 809

March - October

WEST OF ENGLAND

Easewell Farm Holiday Park `14`

Mortehoe, Woolacombe, Devon, EX34 7EH
Tel: 01271 870343
www.woolacombe.com

 max 28 ft

Having driven round the beautifully kept nine hole golf course you arrive at the top of the campsite and can immediately appreciate the sea views that you will enjoy during your holiday. Laid out in terraces the top most camping areas at the entrance command the best views. This is a luxury site with excellent facilities including a heated indoor pool, indoor bowls, snooker, golf, children's play area, restaurant and licensed club.

NA 30   NP 300   16 AMP

WC

Beach 15-20 minutes.

£££

Directions: From the junction of the A361 and B3343 at Mullacott Cross, follow signpost for Woolacombe and Mortehoe. In half a mile turn right at Turnpike Cross signposted Mortehoe. Site is on the right in one mile.

GPS: N51°11.237 W004°12.012'
OS grid: 180 SS 462 455

February - October

Eype House Caravan Park `85`

Eype, Bridport, Dorset DT6 6AL
Tel: 01308 424903
www.eypehouse.co.uk

Approached down a very narrow high-hedged lane, this lovely little south facing steeply sloping terraced site is only suitable for tents and small campervans. The elevated location provides excellent views from every pitch, down to the beach and along a section of the Jurassic coast. There are static caravans for hire below the tent pitches. The pebble beach can be accessed downhill in 200 metres with about 14 steps.

NA 4   NP 20

WC

Pub, shop, beach and slipway at West Bay.

£££

Directions: The site is not licensed for touring caravans. 1 1/4 miles West of Bridport on the A35. Take the turning South to Eype and drive through the village towards the sea.

GPS: N50°43.045'W002°47.043'
OS grid: 193 SY 446 912

All Year

Europa Park

18

Beach Road, Woolacombe, Devon, EX34 7AN
Tel: 01271 871425   www.europapark.co.uk

Ice Cool Camping. Europa Park is a lively, vibrant site with a great atmosphere, with some funky and unique accommodation for hire. This is probably the only campsite in the county that actively encourages Stag and Hen parties. The site is staggering distance from Woolacombe village and beach. There are several toilet blocks, an open all day café and late night bar, a Spar shop by the gate, an indoor pool, sauna, and even a Surfboard Hire Caravan. To top it all there is an awesome sea view towards Lundy, that can be seen from all over this terraced site.

NA 16   NP 300   10 AMP

WC

Pub 300 metres.

Directions: On the B3343 road. The site is on the right hand side of the main road by a garage approximately one mile from Woolacombe.

GPS: N51°10.320'W004°11.030'
OS grid: 180 SS 473 437

February - October

Golden Cap [83]

Seatown, Chideock, Bridport, Dorset,
DT6 6JX Tel: 01308 422139
www.wdlh.co.uk

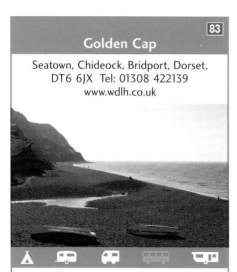

Located perfectly for a beach holiday with easy access to the shingle beach only two minutes walk. It's unfortunate that only from a handful of pitches can a sea view be enjoyed. There are glimpses of sea in some other areas but there are good views of the surrounding hills. A modern toilet block is provided. Pitches are well defined with plenty of shrubs and trees breaking up the site. Levelling blocks are supplied where required and some areas are a little cosy.

| NA 154 | NP 159 | 10 AMP | | |

Pub 100 metres. Slipway 2miles.

£££

Directions: Take the A35 to Chideock. Turn off opposite the church into Duch Street, for Seatown. Follow this road to the coast and the park entrance is on the left just before the car park. This is a narrow lane.

GPS: N50°43.415'W002°49.325'
OS grid: 193 SY 423 920

March - October

Helwell Bay Holidays [5]

Watchet, Somerset TA23 0UG
Tel: 01948 631781
www.helwellbay.co.uk

Helwell Bay is a traditional site occupying a narrow cliff top strip right on the Bristol Channel, with views along the Somerset coastline and across to Wales. The dozen touring pitches at the site entrance do not have quite as good sea views as single line of static caravans that are available for hire. The West Somerset Steam Railway runs just behind. The quaint harbour town of Watchet is five minutes walk and two minutes down onto the beach.

| NA 6 | NP 12 | 10 AMP | | |

Pub 100 metres.

£££

Directions: Drive to Williton on either the A358 from Taunton or A39 and take the B3191 at the bottom of Williton High Street, then turn right at the Masons Arms. Follow to the end and turn left. As you enter Watchet the sea is on your right. Follow the road until you see the Helwell Bay Holidays sign by the second small turning on the right.

GPS: N51°10.863'W003°19.370'
OS grid: 181 ST 077 432

March - November

58
Higher Pentreath Farm

Praa Sands, Penzance, Cornwall, TR20 9TL
Tel: 01736 763222

This site has not been ravaged by the modern world. Simple camping fields and basic facilities are all you need to enjoy this wonderful area. Stunning views are enjoyed from every camping field the higher up you go the better the sea view and the quieter it gets. There is a 15 minute walk downhill to the beach.

| NA | 8 | NP | 100 | 10 AMP |

| WC |

Pub and beach 15 minutes downhill.

£££

Directions: Leave the A30 at the Penzance/Helston roundabout and take the A394 towards Helston. Go over the roundabout and through Rosudgeon. After the signpost for Newtown turn right into Pentreath Lane in front of Jet Garage. The site is at the top of the hill.

GPS: N50°06.422'W005°23.692'
OS grid: 203 SW 574 284

March - October

84
Highland End Holiday Park

Eype, Bridport, Dorset, DT6 6AR
Tel: 01308 422139
www.wdlh.co.uk

The camping fields offer exceptional views, some over rolling hills some over the cliffs to the sea. This site oozes quality and refinement that you can sense as you come down the drive. The bar has wonderful old Royal Berkshire fire engines on display there is also a large formal restaurant. The Heritage Coastline offers wonderful walking and it is just 500 metres downhill to the shingle beach.

| NA | 27 | NP | 192 | 10 AMP |

| WC |

Pub, shop and beach at West Bay.

£££

Directions: Follow the Bridport bypass and take the turning off to Eype. Take the fourth right hand turning which is indicated with a brown sign. Follow this road to the park entrance.

GPS: N50°43.263'W002°46.634'
OS grid: 193 SY 452 913

March - October

Hillhead Caravan Club Site [75]

Hillhead, Brixham, TQ5 0HH
Tel: 01803 853204
www.caravanclub.co.uk

This site stretches the boundaries both in this guide, as so few pitches have a view of the sea but also the level of quality, this is truly an exceptional site. Hedged terraced areas create a more secluded feel. Many of the pitches are serviced hard standings. The communal facilities are second to none and there is a great children's castellated play area. Mansands Beach is a vigorous 2 1/2 mile downhill walk.

| NA | 22 | NP | 239 | 16 AMP | | |

| WC | | | | | MG |

Beach 15 minutes down hill.

£££   WiFi

Directions: At Hillhead turn off A379 onto B3205 signposted 'Kingswear' and 'Dartmouth', signposted 'Lower Ferry'.

GPS: N50°22.207'W003°32.696'
OS grid: 202 SX 904 534

March - January

Ivyleaf CL [25]

Ivyleaf Farm, Bude, Cornwall, EX23 9LD
Tel: 01288 321592
www.ivyleafgolf.com

This is very different CL that really breaks the mould. There are five marked hard standing, serviced bays in a hedged corner overlooking the golf course. The views stretch across countryside to the sea in the distance. Being part of and adjacent to a golf and mountain boarding centre campers can use the toilets, showers and washing machines. Book in at reception on arrival and advanced booking is recommended.

| NA | 1 | NP | 5 | 16 AMP | | |

| WC | | | | | |

££   M   WiFi

Directions: Best approach: Fork left off A39 (Kilkhampton - Stratton) 1 1/2m past Kilkhampton at sharp right bend (see sign Ivyleaf Golf Course). Farm is on right over brow of hill.

GPS: N50°51.129'W004°30.260'
OS grid: 190 SS 241 085

All Year

56 Kemyel Crease CL

Paul, Penzance, Cornwall. TR19 6NP
Tel: 01736 731589
www.caravanclub.co.uk

This is one of those places you would never find on your own. Truly secluded it is an honour to be able to camp here. The ample paddock is slightly sloping but most level around the edges. The sea view is not the most stunning but the environment is. It's so lovely here you can't help but be nice to each other.

NA	2	NP	5

£££

Directions: From Penzance take the A3315 signposted 'Porthcurno'. In 1 1/2 miles fork left signposted 'Castallack', at right bend continue on to 'No through road' and at end bear left. Call at farmhouse on left.

GPS: N50°04.128'W005°33.259'
OS grid: 203 SW 458 247

June - September

57 Kenneggy Cove Holiday Park

Higher Kenneggy, Rosudgeon, Penzance,
Cornwall TR20 9AU Tel: 01736 763453
www.kenneggycove.co.uk

Small and pleasant, this tranquil site has a policy of no noise after 10pm or before 8am. The tropical planting and general landscape make this campsite a lovely garden. Sea views are available but hedge growth could reduce this, though does offer shelter from the wind. A 12 minute walk down a natural footpath brings you to the South West coast path and Kenneggy Sands, a stunning, secluded beach, which is always uncrowded.

NA	4	NP	50	16 AMP

| WC | | | | MG |

£££

Directions: Off the A394. Leave Penzance on A394. After Marazion roundabout look for 'Kenneggy Cove' blue sign between Rosudgean and Kenneggy Downs. Turn off at 'Kenneggy Cove' sign and follow partly unmade road through farm buildings to site. Access tight in places.

GPS: N50°06.495'W005°24.735'
OS grid: 203 SW 562 286

May - November

Ladram Bay Caravan Site

Otterton, Budleigh Salterton, Devon, EX9 7BX
Tel: 01395 568398 www.ladrambay.co.uk

One stop holiday spot. Remotely located this is a big site with lots of quality accommodation and excellent facilities. You really could come here for a week and feel no need to leave site. The private shingle beach is just stunning, you can entertain yourself for days and there is a slipway to the beach with boat storage. The camping fields are terraced with fantastic sea views from most pitches. Indeed sea views can be seen from most places but none better than the bar terrace. There is a very well stocked shop, fantastic children's entertainment and it is directly on the coast path.

| NA | 20 | NP | 200 | 16 AMP | | |

Directions: Turn off B3052 onto B3178 signposted 'Budleigh Salterton'. Turn off signposted 'Ladram Bay' and 'Camping'. Follow signposts to Ladram Bay.

GPS: N50°39.709'W003°17.136'
OS grid: 192 SY 096 851

April - October

Lower Pennycrocker Farm [34]

St. Juliot, Boscastle, Cornwall PL35 0BY
Tel: 01840 250257
www.pennycrocker.com

Spacious and level this cliff top site is part of a working dairy farm in an absolutely beautiful setting. There are good sea views and wonderful views over 15 miles to Padstow and beyond. A new shower block was built in 2008 and new toilets due for 2009. Access to the sea is about a ten minutes drive. From the coast path you can walk to Cornwall's highest cliffs. The on site fishing lakes are stocked with carp and tench.

| NA | 6 | | NP | 40 | | 16 AMP | |

Directions: Turn off A39 sp 'Boscastle onto B3263. Turn off B3263 sp 'Lower Pennycrocker Farm'. Follow signs down narrow, single track road with passing places. Site on left, signed.

AA

GPS: N50°42.212'W004°39.377'
OS grid: 190 SX 125 927

Easter - October

Minehead Camping and Caravanning Club Site [8]

Hopcott Road, Minehead, Somerset,
TA24 6DJ Tel: 01643 704345
www.siteseeker.co.uk

This site is perched high above Minehead on North Hill, part of Exmoor National Park, not every pitch has sea views but what a stunning location. Unfortunately trees are reducing the sea view every year and it is a long walk to the beach or Minehead. Walkers need only walk out of the gate to set foot on the moor and see the ponies.

| NA | 3 | | NP | 60 | | 16 AMP | |

Pub, shop, beach and slipway at Minehead.

Directions: From the A39 either direction, drive to Minehead town centre not to the seafront. At Wellington Square opposite HSBC bank, turn into the High Street (The Parade) and take the second left into Blenheim Road and the next left into Martlet Road. Keep left at the church following a narrow, steep and twisty road for one mile to the site, which is on the right. No Caravans allowed.

GPS: N51°12.834'W003°29.680'
OS grid: 181 SS 958 471

May - September

Mollie Tuckers Field CL
71

East Prawle, Kingsbridge, Devon TQ7 2BY
Enq to; Wincot, Town Road, East Prawle, TQ7 2DF
Tel: 01548 511422 www.caravanclub.co.uk

Just 50 metres from the village green where there are two pubs a shop and café. Stephens field is just round the corner. This is a buzzing place during the summer holidays with Regattas in August, you will need to pre book. Out of season you will be able to relax in peace and quiet and enjoy the wide-open sea view.

| NA | 3/4 | NP | 5 | 16 AMP |

Pub, shop, beach and slipway 20 minutes down hill.

£££

Directions: Drive straight through East Prawle village signposted 'Prawle Point'. Mollies Field in on left through a five bar gate, signed.

GPS: N50°12.871'W003°42.596'
OS grid: 202 SX 780 362

All Year

Mothers Ivey's Bay
37

Trevose Head, Nr Padstow,
Cornwall, PL28 8SL Tel: 01841 520990
www.motheriveysbay.com

This is a big holiday park adjacent to Trevose Golf and Country Club is ideal for a beach holiday, with lots of holiday homes set closest to the sea. The beach (pictured) is just perfect with soft golden sand in a cliff-backed cove. There is a camping field in summer that gives good sea views and there are some excellent serviced pitches. The facilities are superb and a great deal of effort has gone into landscaping this park.

| NA | 25 | NP | 175 | 10 AMP |

Pub at Harlin. Shop and slipway at Padstow.

£££

Directions: Take A39 from Wadebridge turning left at roundabout to Padstow on the B3274. At crossroads in three miles turn left to St Merryn. Turn left at crossroads in St Merryn. Take next right turn (400yds) signposted to Trevose Golf Club'. At the Golf Club turn right on the sharp left hand bend. Turn left at the next junction and Mother Ivey's is second on the right.

GPS: N50°32.473'W005°00.841'
OS grid: 200 SW 865 755

March - October

Napps Camping and Touring Holidays [10]

Old Coast Road, Berrynarbor, North Devon,
EX34 9SW Tel: 01271 882557
www.napps.co.uk

Delightfully located in an area of outstanding natural beauty. This is a really pleasant and quiet touring and tenting only site. The pitching areas are terraced into the hillside providing ever increasingly beautiful views the higher you climb. There is an outdoor heated pool, nice bar and grill, well stocked shop and superb toilets. The sea is only 10 minutes down 220 steps.

| NA 45 | NP 200 | 10 AMP | | |

Pub, shop, beach and slipway 400 metres at Watermouth.

£££

Directions: Two miles South West of Combe Martin three miles East of Ilfracombe on the A399. The site owner advises that you avoid Barnstaple as it is often congested and that you avoid the A39 coastal route from Minehead and Porlock as the road is narrow and extremely steep in parts.

GPS: N51°12.512'W004°03.863'
OS grid: 180 SS 559 479

March - end October

Pebble Bank [90]

90 Camp Road, Weymouth, Dorset,
DT4 9HF Tel: 01305 774844
www.pebblebank.co.uk

Ajacent to Chesil Beach this is a homely and comfortable site. There are 100 static caravans privately owned and rented. Tourers have their own pine tree edged, small, partly sloping area, overlooking, the Fleet with fisherman's huts then onto Chesil Beach. Access to the Fleet is 100m. The one acre tent field at the top of the site has spectacular views across Portland and Chesil Beach.

| NA 5 | NP 40 | 10 AMP |

Pub and shop at Old Wyke.

£££

Directions: Turn Right off the A354 Weymouth-Portland road at the mini roundabout onto the B3156 Wyke Road. In about one mile at a right hand bend just past church into Camp Road, the site is on the left in 500 yards.

AA ▶▶▶

GPS: N50°35.774'W002°29.248'
OS grid: 194 SY 657 776

April - October

North Morte Farm Camping and Caravan Park 17

Mortehoe, Woolacombe, North Devon, EX34 7EG
Tel: 01271 870381 www.northmortefarm.co.uk

Camping here is as it should be, wild but civilised. The site entrance is just off the centre of Mortehoe village, so convenient to shops and restaurants. The camping fields are all well manicured to enable comfortable camping. The sea views are absolutely stunning and the stargazing exceptional. There are modern toilet blocks, serviced touring pitches and static caravans for hire.

Directions: From Barnstable on the A361 signposted Illfracombe. After 10 miles, at Mullacutt Cross roundabout take the first left signposted Morthoe/Woolacombe. Two miles later, take the right turn, signposted Mortehoe. Another two miles on in Mortehoe village turn right, signposted Bull Point lighthouse and North Morte Farm. The site is 500 yards on your left.

NA 25   NP 175   16 AMP

WC

Pub at Mortehoe. Beach 10 minute walk.

GPS: N51°11.301'W004°12.216'
OS grid: 180 SS 461 457

Easter - October

26 Penhalt Farm Holiday Park

Widemouth Bay, Poundstock, Bude,
Cornwall EX23 ODG Tel: 01288 361210
www.penhaltfarm.co.uk

Situated high on the Coastal Downs, a mile South of Widemouth Bay, every pitch has commanding views of the magnificent Atlantic coastline and the beautiful surrounding countryside. This site would be the editor's choice if visiting Widemouth Bay having a preference for open space and simple sites. Two caravans are available to rent. Widemouth Bay is a 10 minute walk, this a popular sandy beach good for surfing and swimming.

NA 4¹/₂   NP   10 AMP

WC

Beach 10 minutes downhill.

£££

Directions: On the A39 from Bude take second turning to Widemouth signposted 'Widemouth Bay Caravan Park'. Follow road until just past the Widemouth Manor pub. Turn left signed 'Mibrook', follow road and Penhalt Farm is on the left. Signed.

GPS: N50°46.393'W004°33.765'
OS grid: 190 SS 194 003

March - October

22 Putsborough Sands

The Anchorage, Putsborough, Georgeham,
Braunton, EX33 1LB Tel: 01271 890230
www.putsborough.com

This two acre site is right alongside an enormous sandy surf beach. The touring caravan only pitches are in an area that is sheltered, gently sloping and parts are terraced. There is no camping for tents on this site and small campervans may be able to park near the beach but will be charged to do so. This is an absolutely perfect site for a beach holiday, especially if you like to surf, sail or windsurf. Surfing equipment is available for hire.

NA 2   NP 25   16 AMP

WC

£££

Directions: Leave Braunton on B231 to Croyde and Georgeham then follow signposts to Putsborough and Sands. Narrow approach road.

GPS: N51°08.614'W004°13.198'
OS grid: 180 SS 448 405

April - September

Pentewan Sands Holiday Park

67

Pertewan, Cornwall, PL26 6BT
Tel: 01726 843485 www.pentewan.co.uk

This large commercial site has everything including its own private sandy beach. The site is mainly level so only the front row has excellent sea views, however from these 48 pitches you can literally roll out of bed and onto the beach, where there is a children's playground and designated swimming and boat areas. Pentewan village is two minutes walk and The Lost Gardens of Helegan are two miles uphill. Advance booking is essential in high season when pitches are available for weekly slots only.

| NA | 32 | NP | 350 | 16 AMP |
| WC | | | | | MG |

Pub, shop, beach, slipway, play area and footpath onsite.

Directions: From St Austell take the B3273. The site is adjacent to this road at Pentewan.

GPS: N50°17.289'W004°47.150'
OS grid: 204 SX 016 468

March - October

Salcombe Regis Camping and Caravan Park [80]

Salcombe Regis, Sidmouth, Devon,
EX10 0JH Tel: 01395 514303
www.salcombe-regis.co.uk

This is a gorgeous medium sized site that really offers quality camping in every aspect. Unfortunately, only a handful of tent pitches benefit from the wonderful valley and sea view. The facilities, grass and park are kept immaculate. Sidmouth about 10 minutes drive retains its Regency and Victorian elegance also having two pebble beaches which, at low tide, give way to golden sand and rock pools.

NA 16   NP   16 AMP

WC

£££

Directions: The park is well signposted on the Exeter-Lyme Regis road (A3052), from both directions. Do not take your caravan into Sidmouth itself. From the east on the A3052, take the first turning left after the Donkey Sanctuary. Follow the road around and you will find us on the left hand side just past the Golf Range.

GPS: N50°41.743'W003°12.307'
OS grid: 192 SY 149 892

March - October

Sandaway Beach Holiday Park [12]

Near Berrynarbor, Ilfracombe, Devon,
EX34 9ST Tel: 01271 866766
www.johnfowlerholidays.com/sandaway-beach.htm

From many of the holiday homes on this park there are excellent sea views, though no view is available from the small touring area. A small tent area amongst trees does have a nice view through a break in the trees. The best views are enjoyed from the bar and as you walk around. Three minutes walk down a picturesque stepped path brings you to Sandaway Beach privately owned by the campsite.

NA 20   NP 20   10 AMP

WC

Pub, shop and slipway 1 1/2 miles at Watermouth Cove.

£££

Directions: On the A399 a quarter of a mile North West of Combe Martin.

GPS: N51°12.377'W004°02.690'
OS grid: 180 SS 571 471

March - November

Sandymouth Bay Holiday Park [29]

Bude, Cornwall, EX23 9HW
Tel: 01288 352563 www.sandymouthbay.co.uk

One of the best sea views in the west. From the touring pitches and 10 acre camping field there are awesome panoramic views of coast and countryside. This is a big family park with lots of quality accommodation, and excellent facilities though due to the location of the camping area, you feel like you are out on your own. The beach is a 10 minute walk.

Directions: Turn off A39 south of Kirkhampton sign posted 'Sandymouth'. Follow road for one mile and after village of Stibb turn left sign posted 'Sandymouth Holiday Park' and 'Sandy Mouth Bay National Trust'. Site on right.

NA 25   NP 50   10 AMP

Pub, shop and slipway at Bude.

GPS: N50°52.012'W004°32.249'
OS grid: 190 SS 217 107

March - September

WEST OF ENGLAND

Seaview International Holiday Park [65]

Boswinger, Gorran, St Austell, Cornwall, PL26 6LL Tel: 01726 843425
www.seaviewinternational.com

This is an exceptional family park that won overall AA Campsite of the Year 2007. There are about seven touring pitches that have a good view of the sea. The sea can also be seen from the pool and children's play area. The beach is about a 10 minute walk down a narrow road or a five minute drive. Advanced booking will be essential if you want to stop at this fantastic site and be guaranteed a sea view pitch.

| NA | 27 | NP | 189 | 16 AMP | | |

| WC | | | | | | | MG | MB |

Beach 10 minute walk.

£££

Directions: Follow signs for lost Gardens of Heligan. Continue past Heligan and Seaview is four miles further on.

GPS: N50°14.219'W004°49.195'
OS grid: 204 SW 990 411

May - September

Sennen Cove Camping and Caravanning Club Site [54]

St. Buryan, Penzance, Cornwall TR19 6JB
Tel: 01736 871588
www.siteseeker.co.uk

This is a small, gently sloping, well maintained site. The sea can be seen over the hedges and attractive farmland. Walking to the beach takes you down a one mile steep path with steps, you can also walk to Land's End on the coast path, where there are pubs, restaurants and amusements. Aircraft noise can be heard on site but can be appreciated if you take a scenic flight in a Cessna. See www.islesofscilly-travel.co.uk

| NA | 3 | NP | 72 | 16 AMP | | |

| WC | | | | | | | MG | MB |

Pub and shop at St Just.

£££

Directions: From St Just head towards Land's End on the B3306, the site is on the right just past Land's End Airport, signed.

GPS: N50°05.381'W005°40.150'
OS grid: 203 SW 375 276

May - September

Slapton Sands Camping and Caravanning Site 73

Middle Grounds, Slapton, Kingsbridge,
Devon TQ7 2QW Tel: 01548 580538
www.siteseeker.co.uk

Hedges and trees obscure what might be an awesome view of the long shingle beach and the amazing Slapton Ley, a long strip of fresh water just behind the beach. Predominantly used by tenters there are only eight touring pitches on this unilluminated site. The beach is accessed downhill on tarmac taking about 20 minutes to walk or a five minute drive, there are sandy beaches at each end.

NA	3		NP	115		16 AMP		

Pub 5 minutes. Shop and slipway at Torcross.

£££

Directions: From A379 turn off in middle of Slapton Ley and beach (inland lake) by memorial signed 'Caravaning quarter of a mile'. Follow road uphill for quarter of a mile and site on right. Signposted 'Slapton'.

GPS: N50°17.439'W003°39.026'
OS grid: 202 SX 825 450

March - November

St. Agnes Beacon Caravan Club Site 47

St. Agnes, Cornwall TR5 0NU
Tel: 01872 552543
www.caravanclub.co.uk

Old quarries seem to naturally convert into great campsites and this site certainly benefits from its long lost industrial past. Situated at the foot of the Beacon there are good views to the Cornish coastline. Much of the site is gently sloping and arranged on several levels, partly sheltered by gorse-topped banking. There is no toilet block but high standards are maintained across the site, which has the usual club feel.

NA	6		NP	112		16 AMP		

Pub and shop at St Agnes.

££

Directions: Right next to Beacon Cottage Farm. From the A30 at Chiverton roundabout take the B3277 to St. Agnes. Turn left as you enter St Agnes. In 1¼ miles over the crossroads, fork right into Beacon Drive. The site is the second tarmac driveway on the right.

GPS: N50°18.448'W005°13.534'
OS grid: 203 SW 705 502

March - September

Staple Farm CL `2`

West Quantoxhead, Taunton, Somerset,
TA4 4EA Tel: 01984 632495
www.caravanclub.co.uk

Situated on the western end of the Quantock Hills this one acre sloping paddock is part of a traditional working farm. There are good views over the Somerset countryside to the Bristol Channel and Minehead located at the foot of North Hill. Most people will find it necessary to make a vehicle journey to go to the sand and shingle tidal estuary beaches.

| NA | 2 | NP | 5 |

Pub and shop 400m.

Directions: Turn left off the A39 Bridgwater to Minehead road at West Quantoxhead immediately past the Windmill Inn. Carry on up this road 250 yards over the crossroads. The farm is in 50 yards.

GPS: N51°09.950'W003°16.495'
OS grid: 181 ST 109 415

Easter - October

Stephens Field `72`

East Prawle, Kingsbridge, Devon TQ7 2BY
Enq to; Wincot, Town Road, East Prawle, TQ7 2DF
Tel: 01548 511422

This summer only camping field has a good sea view but not quite as good as Mollie Tuckers Field that is almost adjacent but will probably be the quietest when things are in full swing and is more sheltered from the South West. There are public toilets by the adjacent village green and there are two pubs a shop and café.

| NA | 4 | NP | 25 |
| WC | | | |

Beach and slipway 20 minutes down hill.

Directions: Drive straight through village signposted 'Prawle Point'. Stephens Field is located at the back left hand side of the village green down an unmade road on left through a five bar gate, signed Stephens field. Booking not necessary.

GPS: N50°12.883'W003°42.593'
OS grid: 202 SX 780 362

July - August

WEST OF ENGLAND

Sunnymead Farm [13]

Mullacott, Ilfracombe, Devon EX34 8NZ
Tel: 01271 879845
http://sunnymead-farm.co.uk

This site offers some of the least expensive camping in the area, which is fair as it is not as well located, there being several sites nearer to Woolacombe and Ilfracombe just three miles away. There are two level paddocks alongside the busy B3343 and these cater for five tourers and plenty of tents with 10 hook ups available. There is a distant view of the sea across farmland.

NA 1 1/2   NP 30   16 AMP

Pub 1 mile.

£££

Directions: Take A361 Barnstaple to Ilfracombe road. At Mullacott Cross take B3343 to Woolacombe. The site is approximately one mile on the right hand side just past the Veterinary Hospital & opposite Highways Guest House.

GPS: N51°10.640'W004°08.793'
OS grid: 180 SS 499 442

Easter - October

Teneriffe Farm [60]

Predannack, Mullion, Helston, Cornwall TR12 7EZ
Tel: 01326 240293

This is a well cared for three acre site. Five of the 24 pitches have a view of the sea so pre-booking is advised. Mullion Cove is within easy walking distance. Mullion village is the largest in Cornwall offering numerous shops and pubs. Polurrian beach is a 1 1/2 mile walk. You can drive five minutes to Polduh and 10 minutes to Kynannace beaches.

NA 3   NP 24   10 AMP

£££

Directions: From the A3083 eight miles South of Helston. Take the B3296 through Mullion towards Mullion Cove, about a quarter of a mile. Turn left, signposted Predannack. Site is on the left in approximately 1 1/4 miles.

GPS: N50°00.290'W005°14.968'
OS grid: 203 SW 672 166

March - January

The Headland Caravan Park `33`

Atlantic Road, Tintagel, Cornwall, PL34 0DE
Tel: 01840 770239
www.headlandcaravanpark.co.uk

Location, Location, Location! Tintagel is just outside the gate where there are many pubs, restaurants, tearooms, local shops and attractions. This is a great rest stop for walkers following the coast path or users of large motorhomes or campers without additional means of transport. There are partial sea views from some areas in this reasonably large mostly level site.

| NA | 5 | NP | 20 | 16 AMP | |
| WC | | | | | |

Slipway at Boscastle.

£££

Directions: Drive straight through Tintagel, following signposts to 'headland' and 'caravan park' and the site is on the right before the headland.

GPS: N50°39.995'W004°45.084'
OS grid: 200 SX 055 887

Easter - October

Tregurrian Camping and Caravanning Club Site `43`

Tregurrian, Near Newquay, Cornwall, TR8 4AE Tel: 01637 860448
www.siteseeker.co.uk

Library picture

A spacious field bordered with hedges, distant views of the sea can been seen from some pitches. A nice site with good views being up to the normal standards of the Camping and Caravanning Club, some pitches have hard-standings. Situated just three quarters of a mile away from Watergate Bay, a glorious sandy beach that is a haven for water sport lovers. There are pretty coastal walks from the site to the beach.

| NA | | NP | 90 | 16 AMP | | |
| WC | | | | | MG | MB |

Pub 1 mile at Trevarrian.

£££

Directions: From the A3059 to Newquay. 1 1/2 miles after passing a service station turn right to Newquay Airport. Continue to a junction where you turn left to Tregurrian and follow the signs to Watergate Bay.

GPS: N50°26.928'W005°02.046'
OS grid: 200 SW 847 654

April - September

Trethias Farm Caravan Park
39

Treyarnon Bay, St. Merryn, Padstow,
Cornwall PL28 8PL
Tel: 01841 520323

This site is meticulously managed which creates a unique atmosphere. Pitches are placed around the edge of the two large fields leaving plenty of space for well behaved children to play. Most pitches have a sea view and it is only a few hundred metres to the beach but there is no vehicle access. The coast path runs close by.

NA	15	NP	63	10 AMP	
WC				MG	MB

Pub 1 mile. Shop, beach and slipway at Padstow.

££

Directions: Off B3276 towards Newquay signposted 'Trethias Farm'. Call at reception by farm in the village, which is a significant distance from the campsite. Max 28ft - if you're brave enough.

GPS: N50°31.365'W005°01.425'
OS grid: 200 SW 856 733

April - September

Trevalgan Touring Park
51

St Ives, Cornwall, TR26 3BJ
Tel: 01736 792048
www.trevalgantouringpark.co.uk

This is the sister site to the excellently located Ayr Holiday Park in St Ives, both are beautifully maintained with excellent facilities. Where Ayr is great for younger campers this site is great for families and people wishing to relax and unwind, there is even a designated area for backpackers. There are views across countryside to sea from many pitches. A bus stops onsite from June - mid September taking campers the two miles to St Ives.

NA	5	NP	132	16 AMP	
WC				MG	

Pub and beach at St Ives. Shop on site.

£££

Directions: Follow B3306 out of St Ives towards Land's End. The site is clearly signed off this road.

GPS: N50°12.468'W005°31.136'
OS grid: 203 SW 490 401

All Year

Treveague Farm Campsite `66`

Gorran, St Austell, Cornwall PL26 6NY
Tel: 01726-842295
http://treveaguefarm.co.uk

Treveague is a family run 200 acre organic working farm, breeding sheep, cattle, and pigs. The four acre partly level campsite is on the brow of a hill. All pitches provide panoramic views across the rolling countryside and sea. There are two well appointed cottages for hire and all guests are encouraged to interact with the farm animals and watch the wildlife from special hides.

| NA 200 | NP 40 | 16 AMP | |
| WC | | | |

Pub and shop 1 mile at Gorran Haven.

£££

Directions: From St Austell follow B3273 turning off at signpost for 'Lost Gardens of Helligan'. Follow road past Lost Gardens and then follow signpost 'Treveague Farm'.

GPS: N50°14.126'W004°48.169'
OS grid: 204 SX 004 413

April - October

Trevean Caravan & Camping Park `44`

St Merrryn, Padstow, Cornwall, PL28 8PR
Tel: 01841 520772

This is a very pleasant small family run campsite on a working farm. From a few pitches there is a distant sea view over countryside. The layout and small number of pitches creates a cosy friendly feel to the campsite. The village of St Merryn is about a mile away as are the golden sands of Porthcothan, Treyarnon and Constantine bays.

| NA 1½ | NP 71 | 16 AMP | |
| WC | | | |

Pub and shop at St Merryn.

££

Directions: Heading towards Newquay on the B3276. After the village of St Merryn turn left signposted 'Trevean Farm'. The site is on the right, signposted. Maximum 25 feet.

GPS: N50°30.742'W004°59.801'
OS grid: 200 SW 874 724

Easter - September

Trevedra Farm Caravan and Camping Site [52]

Sennen, Penzance, Cornwall, TR19 7BE
Tel: 01736 871835/18
www.cornwall-online.co.uk/trevedra/Welcome.html

Trevedra has been a family run site for more than 66 years being part of a working farm. Two fields, one set-aside for Caravan Club members and one field for the general public. There is also a walkers and tent camping field. The facilities are modern and well cared for. Sennen Cove and Gwenver sandy surf beaches are about 15 minutes walk and both have lifeguards in attendance. Land's End is walking distance along the coast path.

| NA 12 | NP 200 | 16 AMP | |

| WC | WC | | | | MG |

Pub, shop and beach at Sennen.

££

Directions: Take the A30 from Penzance to Land's End, pass through the village of Crows-an-Wra, passing the Chapel on your right. Just after the turn off to St Just, B3306, (also on your right), take the first right at the sign to Trevedra Farm.

AA
▶▶▶

GPS: N50°05.282'W005°40.735'
OS grid: 203 SW 369 274

March - October

Trevellas Manor Farm [46]

St. Agnes, Cornwall TR5 0XP
Tel: 01872 552238

Simply perfect and perfectly simple, this camping field gently slopes towards the wonderful sea view and the surrounding rolling countryside is dotted with bygone tin mines. St Agnes, about 1 1/2 miles away, has local shops and restaurants and the beach is a one mile downhill walk away. The simple facilities located by the farmhouse are opposite the entrance to camping field.

| NA 6 | NP 35 | 10 AMP | |

| WC | | | | |

Pub and shop at St Agnes/Mithian.

£££

Directions: Turn off the B3285 to Cross Combe, do not take Airport or School turning. Follow road down to lane with passing places and campsite on the left.

GPS: N50°19.276'W005°11.188'
OS grid: 203 SW 731 517

Easter - September

Trewethett Farm Caravan Club Site 32

Trethevy, Tintagel, PL34 0BQ
Tel: 01840 770222 www.caravanclub.co.uk

Five star site has five star sea view. Perched directly on the Cornish cliffs this immaculately kept site offers fantastic luxury and the sea views are as good as they get. The serviced level touring pitches benefit from being arranged on several terraces, there is even a separate camping field. The sea view is breathtaking from all areas onsite.

Directions: Located directly off B3263 on exiting Tintagel towards Boscastle, signed on left.

NA 15   NP 153   16 AMP

WC

Pub and slipway at Boscastle. Shop at Tintagel.

GPS: N50°40.439'W004°43.606'
OS grid: 200 SX 074 897

March - November

Trewince Farm `63`

Portscatho, Truro, Cornwall TR2 5ET
Tel: 01872 580430
www.trewincefarm.co.uk

This five acre site is part of a working farm, a lovely place with charming owners. Although the site is set out on a slope there are many level pitches. Virtually every pitch offers views of the sea and those with obscured sea views have fantastic countryside views. Towan Beach is within walking distance. Postscartho is a pretty Cornish village just two miles away, with sandy beach, slipway, pubs and restaurants.

| NA | 5 | NP | 25 | 13 AMP | |
| WC | | | | | |

Pub and shop 1 mile at Gorran.

££

Directions: Good access for RVs. From St. Austell take A390 towards Truro. Bear left on the B3287 to Tregony. From Tregony follow the signs to St. Mawes for seven miles to Trewithian and then turn left at the sign for Gerrans, Portscatho, Trewince Manor. Stay on this road, following signs for St. Anthony to Trewince Farm half a mile beyond Gerrans village.

AA
▶▶▶

GPS: N50°09.965'W004°59.327'
OS grid: 204 SW 866 339

May - September

Treyarnon Bay `40`

Padstow, Cornwall, PL28 8JR
Tel; 01841 520681
www.treyarnonbaycaravanpark.co.uk

Adjacent to small but popular sandy beach (pictured), this is a traditional camping and static caravan site. There are several sea views as you move through the park. The camping field has clean porta loos but is set furthest from the beach and shower block. The showers are pay and are also used by beach visitors. The beach is a great place for kids and a lifeguard is in attendance.

| NA | 10 | NP | 55 | 10 AMP | |
| WC | | | | | |

£££

Directions: Follow signpost to 'Treyarnon Bay'. Drive through car park at end of road adjacent to beach. Site entrance in car park. Will accept large motorhomes but access difficult down Cornish lanes - possible but not advisable.

enjoyEngland.com
★★★★
SELF CATERING

GPS: N50°31.660'W005°01.224'
OS grid: 200 SW 858 741

February - October

Warcombe Farm Camping Park [19]

Station Road, Mortehoe, North Devon,
EX34 7EJ Tel: 01271 870690
www.warcombefarm.co.uk

The site gently slopes towards the sea and is split in two by the carp fishing lake. The top half has the best sea views, across the Bristol Channel. Some trees have been planted that may obscure the view in time. The lower part of the park is separated into small hedged areas, from the pitches closest to sea there are glimpses of it over the Devon hedge. The toilet blocks are something else - quite palatial.

| NA | 19 | NP | 260 | 16 AMP |

Pub, shop, beach and slipway at Woolacombe Bay.

£££

Directions: Follow the A361 through Barnstable and follow the signs for Illfracombe until you reach Mullacott Cross Island, 10 miles from Barnstable. Take a left at Mullacott Cross and follow the B3343 towards Woolacombe. After 1³/₄ miles take a right hand turn towards Mortehoe. The park is the first on the right.

GPS: N51°10.771'W004°10.881'
OS grid: 180 SS 478 422

March - October

Warren Bay Holiday Village [6]

Watchet, Somerset, TA23 0JR
Tel: 01984 631460

The site entrance with reception one side and heated indoor pool the other, does not seem to prepare you for the amazing journey to the cliff top camping field. 250 mobile homes are sited on terraces amongst native and exotic trees and shrubs, there are said to be over 200 bird species. The camping field is triangular, the higher you go the better the view. There are very good facilities and a steep path to the private stony and mudflat beach.

| NA | 28 | NP | 150 | 16 AMP |

Pub and shop at Watchet.

££

Directions: 1¹/₄ miles West of Watchet on the B391.

GPS: N51°10.718'W003°21.547'
OS grid: 181 ST 058 430

Easter - October

Warren Farm [7]

Watchet, Somerset, TA23 OJP
Tel: 01984 631220

This campsite is as old as the hills, well not quite but it was established 1928, being part of a 260 acre farm. The site owners are charming and drive around the extensive site in the mornings delivering papers and provisions. Spread over several fields there is always plenty of space, each area offering a different view and feel. There are two toilet blocks though not state of the art, are well maintained and kept immaculately.

NA 14	NP 100	

Pub, shop, beach and slipway at Watchet.

Directions: 1 1/2 miles West of Watchet on the B391.

GPS: N51°10.718'W003°21.547'
OS grid: 181 ST 050 431

Easter - October

West Wayland Touring Park [69]

West Wayland, Looe, Cornwall, PL13 2JS
Tel: 01503 262418
www.westwayland.co.uk

Adjacent to the family farm this is a beautifully kept campsite. The grass is well maintained and unusually level, most pitches offer views across the countryside to the sea. The owners take a great pride in the site and the low tariff represents excellent value for money. There is a beach about one mile away. The pretty seaside town of Looe, with numerous shops, restaurants, pubs and a sandy beach is close by.

NA 20	NP 120	16 AMP	

Pub and shop at Looe.

Directions: Adacent to the A387 in between Looe and Polperro.

GPS: N50°21.117'W004°29.955'
OS grid: 201 SX 223 533

Easter - October

Widemouth Bay Caravan Park [31]

Poundstock, Bude,Cornwall EX23 0DF
Tel: 01288 361208
www.johnfowlerholidays.com/widemouth.htm

This park is big and lively with 50 acres to explore and an abundance of facilities and amenities. The very popular mostly sloping camping area is well away from the main park at the top of the hill. From many of the pitches the sea can be seen but the countryside views are better. Widemouth Bay is a 10-15 minute downhill walk. The sandy beach is very popular and provides good bathing and wonderful surfing.

NA 50   NP 120   16 AMP

WC

£££

Directions: On A39 from Bude head south and take second turning to Widemouth Bay. Turn left past pub/hotel signposted 'Widemouth Bay Caravan Park' and follow road entrance to campsite on left.

GPS: N50°46.594'W004°33.153'
OS grid: 190 SS 198 008

March - October

Windridge CL [88]

481 Chickerell Road, Weymouth, Dorset,
DT3 4DQ Tel: 01305 779268
www.caravanclub.co.uk

An island of tranquillity. This five van site really pulls it out of the bag, it is just wonderful with views all directions. Looking out to sea across Chesil Beach is blissful. Although the site is flanked on one side by a waste transfer site and the other by an MOD firing range, this does not detract from the site which is popular so advanced booking is required.

NA 2   NP 5

Pub, shop and beach at Weymouth.

£££

Directions: Two miles from Weymouth town centre. In between Chickerell and Weymouth at bungalow between Hansen facility and rifle range WRTA Chickerell military site on the main B3157. Signed.

GPS: N50°36.976'W002°30.063'
OS grid: 194 SY 646 797

All Year

Woolacombe Bay Holiday Village [20]

Seymour, Sandy Lane, Woolacombe, Devon, EX34 7AH
Tel: 01271 870343 www.woolacombe.com

© Matt Lenster

This is a large family terraced park with sea views and a wide range of facilities on offer, including: indoor pool, Dunes water park, golf, tennis, bowls as well as relaxation at Club Romano Spa and a lively nightlife. There is a bus to beach and the sister sites. A footpath also leads to the beach. There are lots of holiday homes for hire but this site only takes tents on the camping fields (pictured).

© Matt Lenster

| NA 15 | NP 170 | 16 AMP | |

| WC | | | | |

| | | | | | |

Directions: Turn off the A361 Braunton/Ilfracombe road at the roundabout onto B3343 to Woolacombe. Then follow signs to 'Mortehoe' and 'Woolacombe Bay'.

GPS: N51°10.278'W004°10.478'
OS grid: 180 SS 469 435

All Year

WEST OF ENGLAND

Arthurs Field `64`
Treloan Coastal Farm, Treloan Lane, Portscatho,
The Roseland, Truro, Cornwall, TR2 5EE
Tel: 01872 580989
www.coastalfarmholidays.co.uk/thefarm
Take the A30 from Exeter to Oakhampton and then the
A3076 to Truro. Approximately five miles past Trispen
turn left at signpost A390 to St. Austell through
Tresillian and onto the Probus Bypass. Take the second
turning onto the A3078 signposted Tregony and
St. Mawes. Approximately seven miles past Tregony to
Trewithian turn left signposted Portscatho and Gerrans
to Church. Take Treloan Lane and the site is 300 yards
on the left.

Atlantic View `38`
Trevemedar Farm, St Eval, Wadebridge, Cornwall,
PL27 7UT
Tel: 01841 520431
On the B3276, Padstow to Newquay road 3 1/2 miles
from St. Merryn and three quarters of a mile South of
Porthcothan.

Bagwell Farm Touring Park `87`
Bagwell Farm, Chickerell, Weymouth, Dorset, DT3 4EA
Tel: 01305 782575
www.bagwellfarm.co.uk
In Weymouth, turn West on the B3157 road to
Chickerell. Continue North West for three miles past
the Victoria Inn. Turn left to site.

Bosverbas `59`
Germoe, Near Praa Sands, Penzance, Cornwall.
TR20 9AA
Tel: 01736 762277
East on the A394 road towards Ashton and Helston.
After the Jet Garage at Newtown in 150 yards turn
North onto a private road for 100 yards.

Braddicks Holiday Centre `24`
Merely Road, Westward-Ho, North Devon, EX39 1JU
Tel: 01237 473263
www.braddicksholidaycentre.co.uk
Enter Westward-Ho from the B3236 and turn left or
West along the sea front and the site is on the right
overlooking the sea.

Brea Vean Farm `55`
St. Buryan, Penzance, Cornwall.
Tel: 01736 871318
Take the A30 from Penzance and turn off to St. Just on
the B3306. In about a mile look for the camping site
sign on your left.

Bude Camping and Caravanning Club Site `30`
Gillards Moor, St. Gennys, Bude, Cornwall EX23 0BG
Tel: 01840 230650
www.campingandcaravanningclub.co.uk
From the North on A39 the site is on the right in a lay-
by nine miles from Bude.

Deer Park Holiday Estate `23`
Stoke Fleming, Dartmouth, Devon. TQ6 0RF
Tel: 01803 770253
Two miles South of Dartmouth on the A379, half a mile
North of Stoke Fleming.

East Fleet Farm Touring Park `91`
Fleet Lane, Chickerell, Weymouth, Dorset, DT3 4DW
Tel: 01305 785768
www.eastfleet.co.uk
Three miles West of Weymouth on the B3157 Bridport
road. Turn left at the brown camp site sign down Fleet
Lane for half a mile to the site.

Gwendreath Farm Caravan Park `62`
Kennack Sands, Ruan Minor, Helston, Cornwall,
TR12 7LZ.
Tel: 01326 290666
www.tomandlinda.co.uk
Approaching from Helston on the B3293 pass the
Satellite Earth Station on your right turn right at
crossroads signposted Kennack Sands and Cadgwith.
Turn left in 1 1/2 miles signposted Gwendreath and look
for the sign, Gwendreath Farm Holiday Park

Higher Harlyn Park `36`
St. Merryn, Padstow, Cornwall. PL28 8SG.
Tel: 01841 520022
From Padstow take the B3276 road South West. At the
first cross-roads South of St. Merryn turn right
signposted Harlyn Bay. The site is a third of a mile on
the left.

Higher Tregiffian Farm 53

Sennen Cove Camping and Caravanning Club Club Site,
St. Buryan, Penzance, Cornwall, TR19 6JB
Tel: 01736 871588
Follow the A30 towards Land's End. Turn right onto the
A3306 St. Just/Pendeen Road and the site is 50 yards
on the left.

Home Farm Holiday Centre 3

St Audries Bay, Williton, Somerset, TA4 4DP
Tel: 01984 632487
www.homefarmholidaycentre.co.uk
From the North on the M5 leave the motorway at
junction 24 and take the A39 towards Minehead for 17
miles to West Quantoxhead. After passing
St. Audries Garage on your left take the first road on
your right, the B3191 signposted Blue Anchor Bay and
Doniford. The site entrance is on your right in about
half a mile. The site road is rather long and has several
traffic humps.

Leonards Cove 76

Dartmouth, S.Devon, TQ6 0NR
Tel: 01803 770206
www.leonardscove.co.uk
From the M5 take the A38 signposted Plymouth. Leave
the A38 at Buckfastleigh onto A384 Totnes. Turn right
at traffic lights in Totnes onto the A381 to Kingsbridge.
At Halwell, turn left onto the A3122 to Dartmouth.
From Dartmouth, take the A379 to Stoke Fleming. The
entrance to Leonards Cove is in the middle of the
Village on the left.

Littlesea Holiday Park 89

Lynch Lane, Weymouth, Dorset, DT4 9DT
Tel: 01305 774414
www.havenholidays.com
From Weymouth drive West on the B3157 towards
Chickerell. Just before Granby Industrial Estate turn
South and take the first turning right to Lynch Lane.
The site is at the end of the lane.

Manor Farm Caravan Site 81

Seaton Down Hill, Seaton, Devon, EX12 2JA
Tel: 01297 21524
Seven miles West of Lyme Regis on the A3052 Seaton

road. Turn left at the Tower Filling Station. One mile
North of Seaton.

Mitchums & Myrtle Campsite 21

Moor Lane, Croyde Bay, Devon, EX33 1NN
Tel: 01271 891 046
www.croydebay.co.uk
Tents Only. From Braunton take the B3231 to Croyde.
From Croyde village take Moor Lane.

Mullacott Farm 15

Ilfracombe, North Devon, EX34 8NA
Tel: 01271 866877
www.mullacottfarm.co.uk
Take the A361 from Barnstaple to Ilfracombe. Pass over
the cross-roads where the B3343 bisects the A361 and
the site is about half a mile on your left.

Penhale Caravan & Camping Park 68

Fowey, Cornwall. PL23 1JU.
Tel: 01726 833425
www.penhale-fowey.co.uk
1 1/2 miles South West of Lostwithiel on the A390 St.
Austell road. Turn South East on the B3269 signposted
Fowey, continue to the roundabout one mile from Fowey
then turn right onto the A3082 Par road. The site is on
the left in half a mile.

Penstowe Caravan & Camping Park 28

Kilkhampton, near Bude, Cornwall. EX23 9QY
Tel: 01288 321601
www.hoseasons.co.uk
North of Bude on the A39. Turn left travelling North to
Sandymouth and the site is 200 yards on the right.

Seadown Holiday Park 82

Bridge Road, Charmouth, Dorset, DT6 6QS
Tel: 01297 560145
www.seadownholidaypark.co.uk
From the East take the turning off the Bridport-
Axminster A35 road for Charmouth. In half a mile turn
left into Bridge Road. The site entrance is 100 yards
directly in front. From the West, at the roundabout
West of Charmouth, DO NOT go into Charmouth but
continue on the by-pass for three quarters of a mile and
follow the directions as above.

WEST OF ENGLAND

Slimeridge Farm Touring Park `1`
Links Road, Uphill, Weston Super Mere, Somerset,
BS23 4XY
Tel: 01934 641641
Leave the M5 motorway at Junction 22 and drive North
onto the A38 towards Bristol. Fork left onto the A370
road towards Weston-Super-Mare turning left at Weston
Hospital, Grange Road. Continue and turn right at the
roundabout. Take the first road left, Uphill Way towards
beach and follow the signs to the site which is adjacent
to Weston-Super-Mare beach.

St Audries Bay Holiday Club `4`
West Quantoxhead, Near Watchet, Somerset, TA4 4DY
Tel: 01984 632515
www.staudriesbay.co.uk
From the North on the M5 leave the motorway at
junction 24 and take the A39 towards Minehead for 15
miles towards West Quantoxhead. The site entrance is
on your right just before the village.

St Ives Bay Holiday Park `48`
Upton Towans, Hayle, Cornwall, TR27 5BH
Tel: 01736 752274
www.stivesbay.co.uk
Take the M5 south west at Bristol and then the A30
signposted Oakhampton after Exeter services. Stay on
the A30 for the rest of your journey (until the last half
mile). You will bypass Okehampton, Launceston,
Bodmin, Redruth and Camborne. After Camborne the
road goes through a big dip. At the bottom of the next
hill take the Hayle exit and then turn right at the mini
roundabouts. The park is 500 metres on the left.

Trevornick Holiday Park `41`
Holywell Bay, Newquay, Cornwall. TR8 5PW
Tel: 01637 830531
www.trevornick.co.uk
Three miles South of Newquay on the A3075 on the
Redruth Road. Turn North West to Cubert and
Holywell Bay.

Twitchen Parc `74`
Mortehoe, Woolacombe, Devon, EX34 7ES
Tel: 01271 870343
www.woolacombe.com
Drive South on the A361 Ilfracombe to Barnstaple road

for two miles to Mullacott Cross and turn right on to
the B3343 and follow the signpost to Mortehoe.

Watergate Bay Touring Park `42`
Tregurrian, Newquay, Cornwall. TR8 4AD
Tel: 01637 860387
www.watergatebaytouringpark.eclipse.co.uk
14 miles West of Bodmin on the A30. Turn right after
the railway bridge and follow the signposts for the
airport to the B3276. The site is in half a mile on the
left of this junction.

West Bay Holiday Park `86`
West Bay, Bridport, Dorset, DT6 4HB
Tel: 01308 459491
www.parkdeanholidays.co.uk
From the South East take the M3 from the M25 and
aim for Winchester. From the Midlands and the North
take the A34 towards Westwards towards Bridport. At
the first roundabout take first exit, and at the second
roundabout take second exit into West Bay. The park is
on the right.

Wooda Farm Park `27`
Poughill, Bude, Cornwall. EX23 9HJ
Tel: 01288 352069
www.wooda.co.uk
Turn left off the A39 Wadebridge to Bideford road on
the outskirts of Stratton at the signpost to Poughill and
Coombe Valley. The site is on the right in three quarters
of a mile.

Woolacombe Sands Holiday Park `16`
Beach Road, Woolacombe, Devon, EX34 7AF
Tel: 01271 870569
www.woolacombe-sands.co.uk
Take the North Devon Link Road (A361) from junction
27 of the M5, continue to Barnstaple then following
the signs to Ilfracombe (still A361) through Braunton
then to Mullacott Cross where you turn left on the
B3343 for Woolacombe.

Speedboat, Suffolk

Folkestone, Kent

ENGLAND

PRAWNS
1 PINT
£1.50

OFFER
2 PINTS
£2.50

Reighton Sands, Yorkshire

ENGLAND

Saltburn-by-the-Sea, Yorkshire

Hornsea, Yorkshire

Brighton Pier, East Sussex

ENGLAND

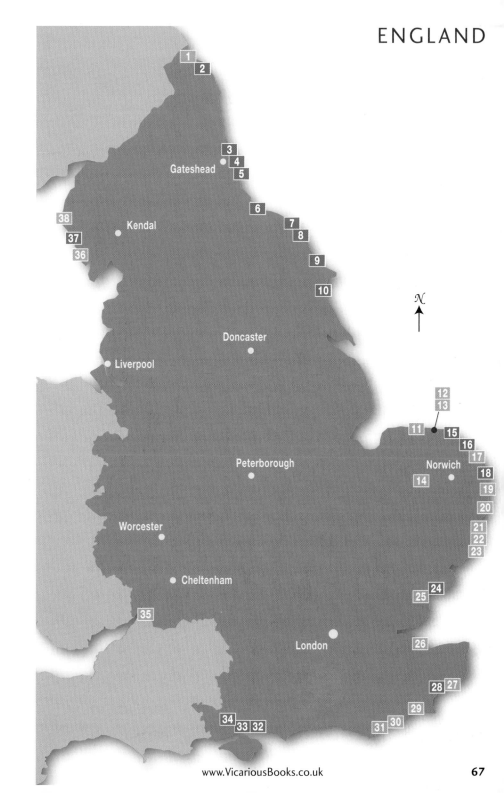

ENGLAND

N

1
2
3
4
5
Gateshead
6
7
8
9
10
38
37
36
Kendal
Doncaster
Liverpool
12
13
11
15
16
17
Norwich
18
14
19
20
Peterborough
21
22
23
Worcester
24
25
Cheltenham
35
26
London
28 27
29
34
33 32
31 30

ENGLAND

Arden CL [33]

Arden, Occupation Lane, Fareham,
Hampshire, PO14 4BZ Tel: 01329 845199
www.caravanclub.co.uk

Arden CL is situated on relatively flat grounds, one mile west of the historic village of Titchfield. The site is quiet and peaceful and has views over fields to the Solent and the busy waterways to Southampton and Portsmouth. There is direct access to footpaths that lead to the Solent, a sand/shingle beach, Meon River and the Titchfield Bird Haven, which are all within walking distance. Close to Ferry Port of Portsmouth for onward travel (return) to France and Spain.

| NA | 3/4 | NP | 5 | 16 AMP | | |

| WC | | | | | MG | MB |

Directions: Leave M27 at Junction 9 onto the A27 Fareham-Portsmouth road. In 1¹/₂ miles at the second roundabout turn right into St. Margaret's Lane. At T-junction turn left into Coach Hill (signposted Titchfield, Fareham). Then immediately turn right into Posbrook Lane (signposted Meon) and in 600 yards turn right at the signpost to Arden into a track. Continue through automatic electric gate, over three speed humps, track then turns right into Arden CL. Set Sat Nav to PO144EZ - Posbrook Lane.

GPS: N50°50.525'W001°14.517'
OS grid: 196 SU 532 052

All Year

Beadnell Bay Camping and Caravan Club Site [2]

Beadnell, Chathill, Northumberland,
NE67 5BX Tel: 01665 720586
www.siteseeker.co.uk

This large and level site is just across the main road from the sea. From site you look straight out to sea, but views are only partial because of the dunes. This site does not accommodate touring caravans nor have electric hook-up.
An alternative site the other side of Seahouses is about a mile away, it is right amongst the Beadnell Bay sand dunes just 20 metres from the sea.
See www.beadnellbaycaravanpark.co.uk
Tel: 01665 720589

| NA | | NP | 150 | 0 AMP | | |

| WC | | | | | MG | MB |

Pub 5 minute walk. Shop 200 yards.

Directions: From the southbound A1 take B1340 signed Seahouses. At Beadnell ignore the village signs and site is on the left just after left hand bend.

GPS: N55°33.675'W001°38.128'
OS grid: 75 NU 231 297

April - October

Crimdon House Farm CS [5]

Coast Road, Hartlepool, Cleveland,
TS27 3AA Tel: 01429 272526
www.siteseeker.co.uk

This is a classic CS. The site has an elevated position and occupies a fairly level three quarters of an acre, well mown field, close to a farm. There are gorgeous, wide views across a large field over the dunes to the sea, which is only a quarter of a mile away and accessible down a National Cycle Way. The site is also at the start of an 11 mile coastal footpath north to Seaham harbour.

NA 1   NP 5   0 AMP

WC

Pub and shop 1 mile.

£££

Directions: From the A19 take the A179 to Hartlepool. At the third roundabout take the A1086 North for Blackhall/Horden. The site is on the right immediately past the green bridge, turn down a farm lane that is easy to miss.

GPS: N54°43.287'W001°15.412'
OS grid: 93 NZ 483 365

All Year

Fen Farm Camping & Caravan Park [24]

East Mersea, Colchester, CO5 8FE
Tel: 01206 383275

This campsite has been family owned for decades and a lot of time, money and thought has been put into improving the site and keeping up with the times. There is an excellent and clean toilet block and an entertaining childs play area. Two large very nicely set out fields offer panoramic views to the sea. There are many walks nearby with the beach being close by and if you really feel fit you could walk the 16 miles around the island.

NA 30   NP 90   10 AMP

WC   MG   MB

Pub 10 minutes. Shop 1 mile.

£££

Directions: From Colchester take the B1052 road for seven miles then East on an unclassified road for about three miles taking a left fork as you come onto the island. Follow the road to the Dog and Phesant pub then take the first turning right.

enjoyEngland.com
★★★★
HOLIDAY &
TOURING PARK

GPS: N51°47.462'E000°59.068'
OS grid: 168 TM 058 144

March - October

ENGLAND

Filey Brigg Caravan and Country Park [9]

North Cliff, Filey, YO14 9ET
Tel: 01723 513852

This Local Authority owned site overlooks the sea. The modern clean and well-kept toilet block has a card entry system. Onsite there is a well-stocked shop and nice café that has a good vegetarian option. The beach is a short downhill walk and you can walk a little further on to Filey where there are plenty of restaurants, bars and shops.

| NA | 9 | NP | 158 | 0 AMP | | |

WC

Shop on site.

£££

Directions: Follow signs from the A165 through Filey to the country park.

GPS: N54°12.865'W000°17.272'
OS grid: 101 TA 118 813

March - October

Fishery Creek Caravan & Camping Park [32]

Fishery Lane, Hayling Island, Hampshire, PO11 9NR Tel: 02392 462164
www.keyparks.co.uk

Library Picture

The Park is set in a beautiful and quiet location adjoining a tidal creek that flows to Chichester Harbour. If you book a creekside pitch you will be able to watch the ebb and flow of the tidal waters or fish from the bankside. There are modern toilet blocks and the site is well laid out with tarmac roads, attractive flowers and shrubs. A five minute walk takes you to an old fashioned seafront with pebbly beach, local shops, restaurants, pubs and clubs.

| NA | | NP | 90 | 10 AMP | | |

WC

Pub and shop 5 minutes.

£££

Directions: From A27 take A3023 (Signed Hayling Island), at first roundabout turn left and follow brown signs to Fishery Creek Park.

GPS: N50°47.055'W000°57.530'
OS grid: 197 SZ 733 987

March - October

Folkestone Camping and Caravanning Club Site [28]

The Warren, Folkestone, Kent, CT19 6NQ
Tel: 01303 255093 www.siteseeker.co.uk

This narrow site is set into the side of the white cliffs of Dover adjacent to a quiet sandy beach. Pitches are well distributed in small groups some having excellent sea views. The local area bears witness to its military past and indeed enhances the opportunities for walking and fishing from the concrete sea defences. Folkestone is a 25 minute hilly walk. The overgrown private access road has parked cars on it all day, often making access even more difficult.

Directions: From the A2 or A20 join the A260 and follow the signs to the Country Park. At the roundabout follow Hill Road. At cross roads drive into Wear Bay Road signposted, 'Martello Tower', site is the fifth on the left.

| NA 4 | NP 80 | 16 AMP | | |

| WC | | | | | | MG | MB |

Pub, shop and slipway at Folkestone.

GPS: N51°05.622'E001°12.372'
OS grid: 179 TR 246 376

March - October

ENGLAND

Hooks House Farm [6]

Whitby Road, Robin Hoods Bay, Whitby,
Yorkshire, YO22 4PE Tel: 01947 880283
www.hookshousefarm.co.uk

© Jill Halder

Situated on a working farm this family run campsite provides a relaxed and pleasant atmosphere for everyone camping. Panoramic sea views of Robin Hoods Bay and countryside views are clearly visible from every pitch. Although shops and pubs are within easy walking distance, the sea is 20 minutes walk down hill. The campsite's owners also offer livery for those wishing to bring their horses.

| NA | 5 | NP | 25 | 10 AMP |

Pub, shop and slipway 1/2 mile at Robin Hoods Bay.

Directions: From Whitby to Hawkser on the A171, then left on the B1447 to Robin Hoods Bay for three miles. The site is on your right.

GPS: N54°26.325'W000°32.575'
OS grid: 94 NZ 945 058

All Year

Old Hartley [3]
Caravan Club Site

Whitley Bay, Tyne and Wear, NE26 4RL
Tel: 0191 2370256
www.caravanclub.co.uk

max 28 ft

This slightly sloping site is perched on a grassy cliff top overlooking the lighthouse on St Mary's Island, a local nature reserve with a bird population of national importance. The views are captivating day and night and if that was not enough, the site is beautifully maintained with excellent facilities. Access to the sea is about five minutes walk and Whitley Bay is about 40 minutes walk.

| NA | 3 1/2 | NP | 64 | 16 AMP |

Pub 500 metres. Shop 1 mile.

Directions: Turn off A19 about three miles North of Tyne Tunnel at junction with A191 (sp Gosforth, Whitley Bay). Follow tourist signs for St Mary's Island, at fourth roundabout turn left onto A1148 (signed Sea Front). At T-junction with A193 at Whitley Bay seafront turn left (signed Blyth), pass Whitley Bay Holiday Park. In two miles at Delaval Arms Pub roundabout turn right onto cycle path. Fork left in 50 yards into site entrance. No outfits over 28ft due to access.

GPS: N55°04.533'W001°27.942'
OS grid: 88 NZ 344 748

January - November

Sandfield House Farm Caravan Park `7`

Sandsend Road, Whitby, North Yorkshire,
YO21 3SR Tel: 01947 602660
www.sandfieldhousefarm.co.uk

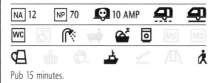

This is one of the few sea view sites that can boast the accolade of being awarded 5 Stars. The grounds are impeccable and there is an attractive stone built, modern central heated amenities block. The park is set in undulating countryside and care has been taken to ensure that all pitches are level. All this and from many of the pitches there are glorious sea views. The beach is within reasonable walking distance and there are walks with glorious scenery and panoramic views of the sea.

| NA | 12 | NP | 70 | 10 AMP | | |

| WC | | | | | | MG | MB |

Pub 15 minutes.

£££

Directions: From Whitby travel one mile North on the A174. The site is on the main road on your left opposite Whitby golf course.

GPS: N54°29.507'W000°38.568'
OS grid: 94 NZ 878 114

March - October

Sandhaven Caravan Site `4`

Bents Park Road, South Shields, NE33 2NL
Tel: 01914 566612
www.northumbrianleisure.co.uk/SandHaven.html

In the heart of the action right by South Shields golden sandy beach, this is a well maintained, high quality site that is largely set to privately owned holiday homes but it does have touring pitches with good sea views. The sea is a short walk and the sandy beaches are perfect for building sandcastles, you can also watch the boats coming and going from the Tyne. You will never be spoilt for choice when it comes to eating out in this cosmopolitan area.

| NA | | NP | 25 | 16 AMP | | |

| WC | | | | | | MG | MB |

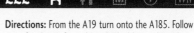

Pub, shop and slipway 5 minutes.

£££

Directions: From the A19 turn onto the A185. Follow signs for the seafront / South Shields Beach until you reach Beach Road. Turn right onto Bents Park Road. The site is just off the beach.

GPS: N54°59.838'W001°25.033'
OS grid: 88 NZ 376 670

March - October

Sandy Gulls Caravan Park **16**

Cromer Road, Mundesley, Norfolk,
NR11 8DF Tel: 01263 720 513
www.ukparks.co.uk/sandygulls

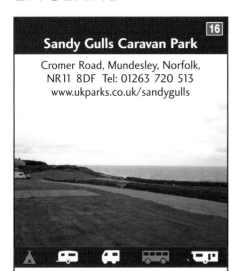

This is a lovely quiet adults only site. Located on a cliff top the sea views are panoramic. Most of the site is occupied with holiday caravans but there is a separate part for tourers with all pitches having great sea views. There is a large clean shower block. A short walk down a slope brings you to the sandy beach which stretches for miles in both directions. Mundesley has been voted one of the country's best kept seaside villages.

NA	16	NP	35	16 AMP

WC					MG	

Pub and shop 1 mile. Slipway in village.

£££

Directions: The site is 6¹/₂ miles South East of Cromer and two miles North West of Mundesley on the B1159 coast road and is best approached from Cromer.

GPS: N52°53.068'E001°25.217'
OS grid: 133 TG 302 379

March - November

Seaside Caravan Park **10**

Ulrome, Driffield, YO25 8TT
Tel: 01262 468228
www.seaside-caravan-park.co.uk

This is a quiet and comfortable site located on a small cliff adjacent to a safe sandy beach. Pitches are large and well spaced, the toilet block adequate and clean. This is the sort of area where little changes from year to year apart from natural coastal erosion. Within walking distance there is a fish and chip shop.

NA		NP	140	10 AMP

WC					MG	

Pub walking distance.

£££

Directions: On the A165 Bridlington/Hull road taking the B1242 to Ulrome where you will see signs to the Seaside Caravan Park.

GPS: N53°59.727'W000°12.742'
OS grid: 107 TA 173 574

March - October

34
Stonehill Farm CL

Calshot Road, Fawley, Southampton,
SO45 1DW Tel: 02380 891442
www.caravanclub.co.uk

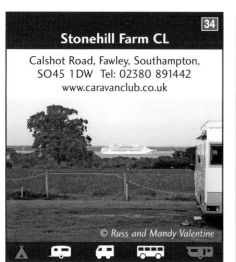

© Russ and Mandy Valentine

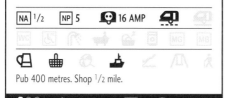

Homely and quiet, this is a level site with some small camping bays. There are fascinating views over Southampton Water with all the busy traffic that sails through it.

NA	1/2	NP	5	16 AMP	

Pub 400 metres. Shop 1/2 mile.

£££   🐕   👥   M   ⓘ   WiFi

Directions: Leave M27 at Junction 2 onto the A326 signposted Fawley and in about 11 miles at the end of the A326 turn left onto the B3053 road signposted Calshot Activity Centre. Within 1 3/4 miles 100 yards past the turn on the left to Ashlett, turn left into a track signposted Stonehill Farm. The site is on the left at the end of the track.

GPS: N50°49.370'W001°20.543'
OS grid: 196 SU 464 028

All Year

37
Tarnside Caravan Park

Tarnside, Braystones, Beckermet,
Cumbria, CA21 2YL
Tel: 01946 841308

A tidy, quiet well mown site that has been made to look attractive with tubs of flowers and a small garden. There are sea views and mountains in the far distance but the sea views are only partial from the touring pitch area. The sandy beach is the other side of the train track, conveniently there is a Train Halt adjacent where one can catch trains to St. Bees.

NA		NP	12	16 AMP	

Pub and shop 1 mile. Slipway 4 miles at St. Bees.

£££   🐕   👥   M   ⓘ   WiFi

Directions: Two miles South of Egremont on the A595. Turn at the sign for Braystones B5345 and follow Caravan Park signs.

GPS: N54°26.537'W003°32.165'
OS grid: 89 NY 005 062

March - October

ENGLAND

The Sheiling CL `18`

Holt road, Cley-next-the-Sea, Holt,
NR25 7TX Tel: 01263 740628
www.caravanclub.co.uk

This is a classic CL of about one acre on a sloping field with panoramic views to the sea and across the Glaven Valley. Access to the sea is about two miles on foot.

| NA | 1 | NP | 5 | 🕱 16 AMP | | |

| WC | | 📶 | | | MG | MB |

Pub at Cley. Shop at Blakeney.

£££ 🐕 ⛄ M ⓘ WiFi

Directions: Turn off the A148 into Holt. In 100 yards at signpost, Cley turn left. The site is on the left in about three miles just after Cley Nurseries.

GPS: N52°56.648'E001°03.303'
OS grid: 133 TG 054 429

All Year

Whitby Holiday Parks `8`

Salt Wick Bay, Whitby, North Yorkshire,
YO22 4JX Tel: 01947 602664
www.whitbypark.co.uk

Overlooking the sweep of Saltwick Bay, this park commands spectacular views of the coastline in a beautifully rural cliff top setting. This is a beautiful, large, tidy commercial site with many static caravans but most of the cliff top area is given over to tourers. There is a steep sandy cliff path to the isolated sand and rock pool beach. There are excellent facilities for all the family. This is a great campsite.

| NA | | NP | 120 | 🕱 16 AMP | | |

| WC | | 📶 | | | MG | MB |

Pub, shop and slipway at Whitby.

£££ 🐕 ⛄ M ⓘ WiFi

Directions: From Scarborough take A171 through Hawkser, turn right following signs to the Y.H.A. The site is on the right two miles down the lane. Final approach road very narrow.

GPS: N54°28.778'W000°35.510'
OS grid: 94 NZ 916 108

March - October

Woodhill Park 15

Cromer Road, East Runton, Norfolk, NR27 9PX
Tel: 01263 512242 www.woodhill-park.com

🛆 · ⛺ 🚐 🚌 🚎 £££ 🐕 👥 Ⓜ ⓘ WiFi

A very impressive site, high up overlooking the sea but close enough to walk into the nearby village. 13 acres are set aside for tourers in three fields, with very pleasantly set out immaculately maintained caravan park and grounds. It's the ideal spot to sit back, relax and take in the inspiring natural landscape.

Directions: On the A148 1 1/2 miles South of Sheringham.

| NA 39 | NP 304 | 16 AMP | | |
| WC | ♿ | 🚿 | 🛁 | 🍽 | ◎ | MG | MB |

Pub 5 minutes.

GPS: N52°56.192'E001°15.722'
OS grid: 133 TG 194 427

March - October

ENGLAND

Abbott's Land Farm `27`
Capel-le-Ferne, Folkestone, Kent, CT18 7HY
Tel: 01303 253564
On the A20 from Dover to Folkestone. Turn off on
B2011 Dover road where Capel-le-Ferne is signposted.

Azure Seas Caravan Park `19`
The Street, Corton, Nr Lowestoft, Suffolk. NR32 5HN
Tel: 01502 731403
www.azureseas.co.uk
From the A12 four miles North of Lowestoft, seven miles
South of Yarmouth. Turn East at the end of a dual
carriageway along Corton Long Lane. The site is
opposite at the junction with 'The Street', Corton, next
to a pub called the Corton Hut.

Bay View Caravan and Camping Park `31`
Old Martello Road, Pevensey Bay, East Sussex.
BN24 6DX
Tel: 01323 768688
www.bay-view.co.uk
Situated next to the beach off the A259 between
Pevensey Bay and Eastbourne.

Cliff Farm CL `35`
Aust, Bristol, Gloucester, BS35 4BG
Tel: 01454 632400
www.caravanclub.co.uk
Leave the M48 at Junction one onto the A403
Avonmouth road and in 100 yards turn right across the
dual carriageway. In about 150 yards past a CL on the
left, turn right over a cattle grid into the drive. The site
entrance to Cliff Farm is at the end.

Cliff House Caravan Park `21`
Sizewell Common, Suffolk, IP16 4TU
Tel: 01728 830724
www.cliffhousepark.co.uk
From Leiston follow the signs to Sizewell.

Cliff House Holiday Park `22`
Minsmere Road, Dunwich, Saxmundham, Suffolk,
IP17 3DQ
Tel: 01728 648282
www.cliffhouseholidays.co.uk
From the A12 at Yoxford, turn left through Westleton to
Dunwich. Approaching Dunwich turn South into

Minsmere Road signposted Dunwich Heath where you
will see a caravan site sign.

Incleboro Fields Caravan Club Site `11`
Station Close, West Runton, Cromer, Norfolk,
NR27 9QG
Tel: 01263 837419
www.caravanclub.co.uk
From Cromer on the A149 turn left in West Runton
opposite the village inn signposted for the Shire Horse
Centre. Within a quarter of a mile immediately past the
railway bridge turn left at the 30 mph speed limit sign
into Station Close.

Manor Farm `12`
Manor Farm, East Runton, Cromer, Norfolk, NR27 9PR
Tel: 01263 512858
www.manorfarmcaravansite.co.uk
Leave the A148 at the Sheringham turn. Turn right at
the roundabout in Sheringham towards West and East
Runton. After a few miles turn right at the brown Manor
Farm Camping sign in East Runton. You will go under a
railway bridge, past the pond and soon after you will
see the entrance to Manor Farm on your left.

Priory Hill Holiday Parks `26`
Wing Road, Leysdown, Sheppey, Kent, ME12 4QT
Tel: 01795 510267
www.prioryhill.co.uk
Take the M20 from London to the A249 signposted to
Sheerness, then take the B2231 road to Leysdown on
Sea.

Ravenglass Camping and Caravan Club Site `36`
Ravenglass, Cumbria, CA18 1SR
Tel: 01229 717250
www.siteseeker.co.uk
From the A595 turn West for Ravenglass. The site is
signed on the left before entering the village.

Rye Bay Caravan Park `29`
Pett Level Road Winchelsea Beach East Sussex,
TN36 4NE
Tel: 01797 226340
On the A259 two miles west of Rye in Winchelsea
village take road signed Winchelsea Beach, site on left
in about three miles.

Seacote Park   38
St Bees, Cumbria CA27 0ET
Tel: 01946 822777
www.seacote.com
Leave the M6 at junction 40 and take the A66 west for approximately 35 miles. Take the A595 towards Whitehaven. Keep on the A595, by-passing the town center. Go through two sets of traffic lights to a roundabout which you go straight over. Then take the second right signposted for St Bees. At the T-Junction at the top of the hill turn left onto the B5345 towards St Bees. Follow the signs to the beach.

Seacroft Caravan Club   13
Runton Road, Cromer, Norfolk, NR27 9NJ
Tel: 01263 511722
www.caravanclub.co.uk
A well signposted site on the A149 Runton Road half a mile West of Cromer.

Seaview Caravan Club Site   1
Billendean Road, Spittal, Berwick-Upon-Tweed, Northumberland, TD15 1QU
Tel: 01289 305198
www.caravanclub.co.uk
From the South on the A1 at the roundabout on the outskirts of Berwick, turn right onto the A1167 signposted Scremerston, Tweed Mouth and Spittal. In 1¼ miles at a roundabout turn right into Billendean Terrace signposted Spittal. There is a sign on the right pointing you towards the site which is in half a mile past a railway bridge.

Shear Barn Holiday Park   30
Barley Lane, Hastings, Sussex. TN35 5DX
Tel: 01424 423585
www.shearbarn.co.uk
Leave the M25 at Junction 5 and follow the A21 all the way to Hastings. Follow the signs to the seafront and turn left. Follow the road round to the Stables Theatre and turn right onto Harold Road. Turn right into Gurth Road, carry on up the hill onto Barley Lane and reception is on your right.

The Manor Caravan Site   17
Happisburgh, Norfolk. NR12 0PW
Tel: 01692 652228

From Stalham take the B1159 towards Walcott on Sea. After approximately four miles take the right hand turn onto the B11590 signposted Happisburgh. Approaching the village with the church on your left, proceed straight ahead uphill to the Hill House Public House. Take the gravelled track to the right hand side of the building and the sea and the camp is straight ahead.

The Vulcan Arms CL   23
Sizewell, Leiston, Suffolk, IP17 1UY
Tel: 01728 830748
www.caravanclub.co.uk
Turn off the A12 onto the B1121 signposted Saxmundham. The site is 10 miles North of Woodbridge and within 1½ miles of Saxmundham. Turn right into the B1119 signposted Leiston and continue through the town following the signpost to Sizewell and the site is on the right within two miles.

Waldegraves and Leisure Park   25
Mersea Island, Colchester, Essex, CO5 8SE
Tel: 01206 382898
From Colchester take the B1025 for 10 miles then fork left towards Mersea Island. Take the second road on the right and follow the signs.

West Runton Camping and Caravanning Club Site   14
Holgate Lane, West Runton, Norfolk, NR27 9NW
Tel: 01263 837544
www.siteseeker.co.uk
On the A148 from Kings Lynn, approaching from West Runton turn left at the Roman Camp Inn into the entry track which is half a miles long and is right at the crest of a hill opposite a National Trust sign. Site Access is rather steep and narrow so drive with care.

White House Beach Caravan Club Site   20
Kessingland, Lowestoft, Suffolk, NR33 7RW
Tel: 01502 740278
www.caravanclub.co.uk
From the North follow the Kessingland by-pass to a roundabout at the end of the dual carriageway and turn left into Whites Lane, signposted Kessingland Industrial Estate and Wild Life Park. Continue into Church Road. In about 1 mile at the sea front, ignoring the 'No Through Road' signs, turn right into Beach Road and the site is on the left.

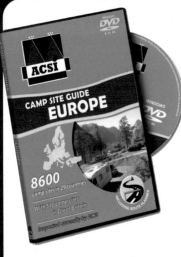

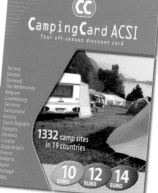

Achnahaird, Ross-shire

SCOTLAND

John O'Groats, Caithness

© Alf Alderson, www.alfalderson.co.uk

SCOTLAND

Highland Cow

Scottish Coastal Ruin

SCOTLAND

Eilean Donan Castle, Dornie

Fishing Nets

SCOTLAND

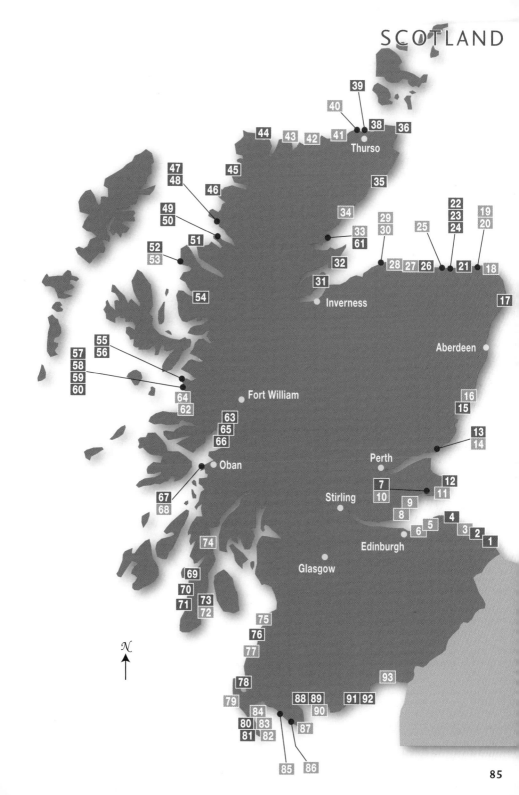

SCOTLAND

Thurso

Inverness

Aberdeen

Fort William

Perth

Oban

Stirling

Edinburgh

Glasgow

N

85

SCOTLAND

Ardmair Point Caravan Park 47

Ardmair, Ullapool, Highlands, IV26 2TN
Tel: 01854 612054
www.ardmair.com

Occupying a small peninsula with a curved pebble bay. This site is set amongst spectacular Highland scenery with the dramatic Ben Mhor Coigach mountain ridge as the backdrop for the sheltered sea loch. There is self-catering accommodation, touring and camping pitches all with spectacular views and great facilities nearby.

| NA | 8 | NP | 50 | 10 AMP | | |

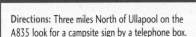

Pub 3 miles. Boat launching from site.

£££

Directions: Three miles North of Ullapool on the A835 look for a campsite sign by a telephone box.

GPS: N57°56.022'W005°11.787'
OS grid: 19 NH 109 983

April - September

Ardwell Caravan Park 80

Ivy Cottage, Ardwell, Dumfries & Galloway, DG9 9LS
Tel: 01776 860291

With superb views of the Irish Sea and Luce Bay this is a very pleasant, simple, level site. Pitches are on the waters edge with firm ground and a hardcore road runs through the site. Facilities onsite are basic and site fees are inexpensive.

| NA | | NP | 25 | 0 AMP | |

Shop at Sandhead. Slipway 1/2 mile.

£££

Directions: From Glenluce take the A7084 to Ardwell. Look carefully for site notice on the right towards the end of the village.

GPS: N54°46.245'W004°56.457'
OS grid: 82 NX 108 456

March - October

Auchenlarie Holiday Park

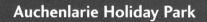

89

Gatehouse of Fleet, Dumfries and Galloway, DG7 2EX
Tel: 01557 840251   www.auchenlarie.co.uk

🏕 🚲 🚐 🚌 🚃 £££ 🐕 🚻 Ⓜ ⓘ WiFi

This is a very large, beautifully maintained holiday park with extensive excellent facilities making it a high quality all singing and all dancing holiday destination. The touring area is high up with beautiful sea views. Hard standings are available all of which are level and there are also some Super pitches. The site has its own sandy, sheltered cove reached by a wide, gravel, and gently sloping cliff path.

NA   NP 70   16 AMP   🚐 🚐
WC   ♿ 🚿 🛁 🚰 MG MB
🔌 🧺 🔍 ⛴ 🏊 🛝 🚶

Directions: From Dumfries follow A75 Stranraer until the sign 'Gatehouse of Fleet'. Continue past town for five miles, the Holiday Park is on the left.

GPS: N54°30.623'W004°16.810'
OS grid: 83 NX 536 522

All Year

SCOTLAND

Badrallach `50`	Banff Links Caravan Park `22`
Croft 9 Badrallach, Dundonnell, Ross-shire, IV23 2QP Tel: 01854 633281 www.badrallach.com	Banff, Aberdeenshire, Grampian, AB45 2JJ Tel: 01261 812228 www.aberdeenshire.gov.uk/caravanparks/locations/banff.asp

This is a beautiful, peaceful and tranquil, small family run site. The owners are romantic about the remoteness and still offer spring water and gas lights. The sea view is only partial once pitched, but they are very fine from the shore or the road. There is no chemical disposal point or TV reception.	Perfectly located this level site is right next to Banff village with its amenities. Some static's and 28 touring pitches are right on the waterfront on the top of the pebble bank. When the tide is out a large sandy beach is exposed, great for children and Boyndie Bay is a popular surfing spot

NA 45 NP 19 16 AMP	NA 3¹/₂ NP 62 10 AMP
Pub 8 miles. Shop 14 miles. Walkers welcome.	Slipway at Bannf.

£££	£££

Directions: Turn left off A835 at Braemar Junction (12 miles south of Ullapool) onto A832, in 11 miles turn right at sign for Badralloch and follow single track road for about eight miles, site on left.	**Directions:** A quarter of a mile off the A98 road one mile West of Banff. Follow signposts to the site which is on the seashore.

GPS: N57°52.407'W005°15.722' **OS grid:** 19 NH 065 915	**GPS:** N57°40.152'W002°33.210' **OS grid:** 29 NJ 673 645
All Year	**April - October**

Blackpots Cottages CS `21`

Whitehills, By Banff,
Aberdeenshire, AB45 2JN
Tel: 01261 861396

This small, level lawned paddock provides terrific sea views. The site is surrounded by a low stone wall which obscures the adjacent road from view when looking out across to the narrow rocky beach to the sea. There is a Fishmongers and a fish and chip shop in the village.

| NA | 0.75 | NP | 5 | 0 AMP | |

Beach adjacent. Slipway in village.

£££

Directions: 2 1/2 miles West of Banff in Whitehills village. Continue past a small harbour and around the corner from a permanent caravan site.

GPS: N57°40.823'W002°34.230'
OS grid: 29 NJ 662 658

April - October

Broomfield Holiday Park `48`

Shore Street, Ullapool, Highlands, IV26 2SX
Tel: 01854 612020
www.broomfieldhp.com

Right on the banks of Lochbroom where you look out to the Summer Islands and Hebrides from the site. Situated in an outstanding environment with wonderful scenery and amazing sunsets yet Ullapool is just behind the site. There is still a major fishing fleet in Ullapool, so visitors can enjoy the comings and goings of the boats and the bounty that they bring home.

| NA | 11 | NP | 140 | 16 AMP | |

Slipway in town.

£££

Directions: In Ullapool continue along Shore Street and take the second right after the harbour where you will see a wide site entrance on the left.

GPS: N57°53.657'W005°09.887'
OS grid: 19 NH 125 938

Easter - September

SCOTLAND

Bunree Caravan Club Site [63]

Onich, Fort William, PH33 6SE
Tel: 01855 821283
www.caravanclub.co.uk

On the waters edge of Loch Linnhe with sea and mountain views this is a very attractive Caravan Club site where non members are also welcome. Mature trees give a wonderful natural feel to this well managed site. There is a bus stop just 300 metres from site for the Fort William bus.

NA	7	NP	99	16 AMP		
WC						MG

Shop 1¹/₂ miles.

£££

Directions: Turn left off A82 (Glencoe-Fort William) one mile past Onich at Caravan Club sign on to a narrow track with traffic lights.

GPS: N56°42.925'W005°13.750'
OS grid: 41 NN 019 626

March - January

Camusdarach Campsite [56]

Camusdarach, Arisaig, Inverness-shire,
PH39 4NT Tel: 01687 400221
www.camusdarach.com

Absolutely pristine facilities and this site is also managed in a environmentally responsible manner, but sadly the sea view is only partial. The grounds are very well cared for and the many large mature trees provide shelter. A footpath from site gives access to the superb sandy beaches, which are a mere three minute stroll. The beach is also licensed for weddings.

NA		NP	42	16 AMP		
WC						MG

Pub 3 miles. Shop 4 miles.

£££

Directions: On the A830 Fort William-Mallag road turn left onto B8008 at Arisaig. Site signed in approx four miles on the left.

GPS: N56°57.262'W005°50.782'
OS grid: 40 NM 654 894

March - October

Carradale Bay Caravan Park

73

Carradale, Kintyre, Argyll, PA28 6QG
Tel: 01583 431665 www.carradalebay.com

© Colin Burgess

The park is on a mile long south facing sandy beach backed by dunes. Landscaping provides small camping areas protected by shrubs and bushes, each pitch having good sea views. Situated in an area of outstanding natural beauty this site is suitable for families as there is plenty of walking and cycling in the adjacent Forestry Commission land. This park is highly graded by the Scottish Tourist Board, and winner of the Best Caravan and Camping Park Tourism Award, plus an AA award for Attractive Environment for five years running.

© Colin Burgess

| NA | | NP | 90 | 10 AMP | | |
| WC | | | | | MG | MU |

Pub 15 minutes. Shop 1 mile.

Directions: Site is situated half way between Claonaig and Campbeltown on the B842 (single track road). For large outfits, A83 to Campbeltown then B842 to Carradale.

GPS: N55°35.218'W005°29.482'
OS grid: 69 NR 803 373

Easter - September

SCOTLAND

Castle Point Caravan Site [91]

Rockcliffe, By Dalbeattie,
Dumfries and Galloway, DG5 4QL
Tel: 01556 630248

Real Scottish sea, islands and mountain views are enjoyed from the site, which is very well maintained, clean and tidy. A fairly steep and rough path takes you to a small cove near Castle Point. The 10 minute walk to the point has exciting views of the sea and there are good walks in the area and a safe interesting beach in the village about one mile away.

NA 3	NP 15	16 AMP		
WC				

Pub 1/2 mile. Shop 1 mile.

£££

Directions: From Dalbeattie take the A710 coastal road. After five miles turn right along the road signposted to Rockcliffe. At the brow of the hill just on entering Rockcliffe turn left and drive down to the end of Barclay Road and straight ahead up a private farm road.

Scottish TOURIST BOARD ★★★★ HOLIDAY PARK

GPS: N54°51.565'W003°47.065'
OS grid: 84 NX 855 532

Easter - October

Cullen Bay Caravan Park [24]

Logie Drive, Cullen, Banffshire, AB56 4TW
Tel: 01542 840766
www.cullenbayholidaypark.co.uk

Cullen Bay Park is a very neat and well cared for level site with caravan holiday homes and tourers with an interesting view across the bay. There are some hard-standings with sea views. There are coastal walks in the area and it is about a 20 minute walk to the sea. Bottle nose dolphins are often seen from the cliffs. Cullen town is a 10 minute walk from the site.

NA 5	NP 35	15 AMP		
WC				MG	MB

Pub and shop 10 minutes walk. Slipway at Cullen Harbour.

£££

Directions: In Cullen off the A98 road and follow signposts to the site.

Scottish TOURIST BOARD ★★★★ TOURING PARK

GPS: N57°41.623'W002°48.795'
OS grid: 29 NJ 495 683

April - October

Culzean Castle Camping & Caravanning Club Site [76]

Culzean, Maybole, Ayrshire, KA19 8JX
Tel: 01655 760627
www.siteseeker.co.uk

The site is in the grounds of the magnificent Culzean Castle with good views across arable fields to the sea. The mountains of the Isle of Arran create the horizon and spectacular sunsets can be enjoyed. The sea is about 2^1/$_2$ miles by road. A range of events are held at Culzean Castle, which is open to the public.

NA	600	NP	90	10 AMP		
WC					MG	MB

Pub 4 miles. Slipway 2^1/$_2$ miles.

£££

Directions: From A77 Girvan to Maybole road at Turnbury take A719. Site signed on the left in approximately three miles.

Scottish TOURIST BOARD
★★★★
TOURING PARK

GPS: N55°21.213'W004°46.180'
OS grid: 70 NS 247 099

March - October

Dunbar Camping & Caravanning Club Site [2]

Oxwellmains, Dunbar, East Lothian, EH42 1WG Tel: 01368 866881
www.siteseeker.co.uk

Library Picture

This site was purpose built, opened in September 2008 with all new facilities and amenities. There are views of the sea from most of the site and pitches. The sea is about an eight minute walk. Dunbar town about seven miles away has several places to eat out. Close by are a wildlife reserve and a geological trail.

NA		NP	90	10 AMP		
WC					MG	MB

Shop at Dunbar.

£££

Directions: Leave A1 south of Dunbar (DO NOT ENTER DUNBAR) on to A1087 and cross over railway and take road on right site signed.

GPS: N55°59.693'W002°28.812'
OS grid: 67 NT 700 780

April - November

Dunnet Bay Caravan Club Site 38

Dunnet, Thurso, Caithness, KW14 8XD
Tel: 01847 821319 www.caravanclub.co.uk

Å   🚐   🚙   🚌   🚐   £££   🐕   ††   M   ⓘ   WiFi

Many pitches have glorious views of the sea through sand dunes, and some are right next to the beach. Solitude can be enjoyed here whilst you look out over uninterrupted clean washed sands to Dunnet Head, the northernmost point of the mainland of Britain. Climbing Dunnet will reward you with magnificent views over the Pentland Firth to Orkney, Ben Loyal and Ben Hope. Units over 28 feet should contact site in advance.

| NA | 5 | NP | 57 | 🔌 16 AMP |
| WC | ♿ | ☂ | | 🚿 | 🔵 | MG | MB |

Pub ¹/2 mile. Shop 2¹/2 miles. Boats can be launched from beach.

Directions: From the East (John O'Groats) A836 site on right in half mile past Dunnet village.
From the West (Thurso) on A836 site on left approx 2¹/2 miles past Castletown village.

Scottish TOURIST BOARD ★★★★★ TOURING PARK

GPS: N58°36.927'W003°20.672'
OS grid: 12 ND 219 705

April - October

Findochty Caravan Park

26

Jubilee Terrace, Findochty, Buckie, Banffshire, AB56 4QA
Tel: 01542 835303 www.findochtycaravanpark.co.uk

This is a great, compact site built into a rocky hollow looking out over the small shingle beach. Conveniently located the local pub is next door and the 100 berth harbour of the interesting little town of Findochty is adjacent. This park is of approximately three acres and has mobile homes for hire. There are 30 touring pitches under the cliffs, 20 of which have electric. There are good views of the Moray Firth where dolphins are seen almost daily.

Directions: On the A98 road two miles East of Buckie. Drive to Findochty harbour and turn left.

NA 3   NP 30   16 AMP

WC

GPS: N57°41.890'W002°54.452'
OS grid: 28 NJ 459 679

March - October

SCOTLAND

Fortrose Caravan Site [31]

Wester Greengates, Fortrose,
Ross-shire, IV10 8SD
Tel: 01381 621927

The site's location on the shoreline of the loch provides panoramic, interesting views across the Moray Firth with moored sailing craft, the distant hills and a suspension road bridge. This is a beautiful site that is part level and part sloping, a quiet road runs behind it. A network of footpaths provide for interesting walking around the Black Isle and Chanonry Point where dolphins may be seen.

| NA | | NP 50 | 16 AMP | |
| WC | | | | MG | MB |

Shop 10 minute walk. Slipway in harbour.

£££

Directions: A832 to Fortrose. Turn right opposite the Bank of Scotland into Academy Street and site on right in approximately 500 metres.

GPS: N57°34.723'W004°07.107'
OS grid: 27 NH 734 564

April - September

Gairloch Caravan & Camping Holiday Park [52]

Strath, Gairloch, Wester Ross, Highlands,
IV21 2BX Tel: 01445 712373
www.gairlochcaravanpark.com

The Park looks out to the Isle of Skye and West to the outer Hebrides. Across the loch lie the mountains of the Torridon Forest creating a magnificant landscape. All sorts of amenities are right on the doorstep and the sea is just across the road. There are some hard standing pitches, two static caravans and a cottage for hire.

| NA 10 | | NP 63 | 16 AMP | |
| WC | | | | | |

Shop adjacent. Slipway 2 miles.

£££

Directions: Turn West off the A832 in Gairloch onto the B8021. After half a mile turn right immediately after the Millcroft Hotel, the site is on your right.

GPS: N57°43.883'W005°42.172'
OS grid: 19 NG 797 774

April - October

59
Gorten Sands Caravan Site

Gorten Farm, Arisaig, Inverness-shire,
Highlands, PH39 4NS
Tel: 01687 450283

Next to a white sandy beach, this is a very pleasant small site with good facilities and wonderful views. The shoreline is rocky and should make for interesting snorkling and fishing. The campsite is part of the Macdonald family working hill and coastal farm, where traditional harvesting methods are employed.

NA	6	NP	45	6 AMP		
WC						

Pub ³/₄ mile. Shop 2 miles. Small boats on site.

££

Directions: On the A830 Fort William-Mallaig road. Turn left onto B8008 at Arisaig. Turn left at Back of Keppoch and follow road for approx one mile to the end and site entrance.

GPS: N56°55.398'W005°51.548'
OS grid: 40 NM 643 878

May - September

61
Grannie's Helian Hame

Embo, Dornoch, Sutherland,
Highlands, IV25 3QD Tel: 01862 810383
www.parkdeanholidays.co.uk

This large family site is part of the Parkdean Holidays group and it has loads of facilities and entertainment all set amongst the sand dunes. There is a large play area, adventure playground, indoor heated pool and bar with entertainment. The touring pitches are located around the edge of the site with plenty of space and many of those with the electric hook-ups are right on the edge of the beach. The site is also within walking distance to a small village.

NA	5	NP	185	13 AMP		
WC					MG	MB

Slipway on site.

£££

Directions: A9/A949 road to Dornoch. Take the unclassified road North for 2¹/₂ miles and turn right into Embo.

GPS: N57°54.463'W003°59.825'
OS grid: 21 NH 818 926

March - October

SCOTLAND

Gruinard Bay Caravan Park

Laide, Wester Ross, Highlands, IV22 2ND
Tel: 01445 731225
www.gruinard.scotshost.co.uk

This is a small well cared for family run site that is located adjacent to the beach in the village of Laide. The ruins of the Chapel of Sand are adjacent to the Park and add real atmosphere to the setting and there are uninterrupted sea views from the campsite. You can walk two miles down a track from Laide to the ruins of Slaggan where there is also a superb beach nearby.

NA 3¹/₂   NP 40   10 AMP

WC   MG   MB

Pub 2¹/₂ miles. Slipway 1 mile.

£££

Directions: The site is situated on the A832 (Gairloch/Ullapool) road just past the village of Laide.

GPS: N57°51.997'W005°32.193'
OS grid: 19 NG 906 918

April - October

Hillhead of Craichmore CL

Leswalt, Stranraer,
Dumfriesshire & Galloway, DG9 0PN
Tel: 01776 870219

Enclosed within stonewalls and trees lies an attractive, fairly level, glorious, traditional, peaceful C.L. There are fine views across the Loch Ryan. You can sit and watch ferries going to and from Stranraer and it is about a quarter of a mile from the shingle beach.

NA ¹/₄   NP 5   10 AMP

Pub 3 miles. Shop Stranraer. Slipway 1¹/₂ miles.

£££

Directions: Leave Stranraer on the A718 Stranraer-Kirkcolm road. In two miles turn right at the roundabout and in about a ¹/₄ of a mile turn right into the farm road

GPS: N54°55.873'W005°04.290'
OS grid: 82 NX 033 640

All Year

Inver Caravan Park 35

Houstry Road, Dunbeath, Caithness,
KW6 6EH Tel: 01593 731441
www.inver-caravan-park.co.uk

Invercaimbe 55
Caravan & Camping Site

Arisaig, Inverness-shire, PH39 4NT
Tel: 01687 450375
www.invercaimbecaravansite.co.uk

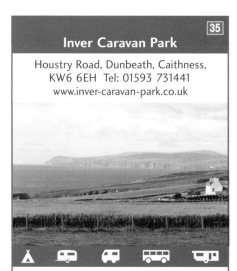

Photo campsite owner

There is a very good sea view from the front row of this site and there are also good views towards the hills. This is a small well kept site with simple but good facilities. It is situated quite high above the sea, a 5-10 minute walk can be taken down a rather steep path to the beach. A longer walk of about a quarter of a mile will give you an easier descent. The beach is rather pebbly with interesting rock pools to explore. Puffins can be seen from walks up the Dunbeath Strath.

Invercaimbe is a West Highland working croft where traditional hill cattle and working highland ponies have been bred for 150 years. A lovely little site spread across a couple of acres, most of which is uneven. It is best to check before booking to make sure that a suitable pitch is available. This is a nice basic site with wild views of the mountains behind it and a lovely safe beach in front. Boat trips can be taken to all the inner Hebridean islands.

| NA 1 | NP 15 | 16 AMP |
| WC | | |

Pub 350 metres. Shop 1/2 mile. Slipway in village.

| NA 2 | NP 20 | 10 AMP |
| WC | | |

Pub 1/2 mile. Shop 1 mile.

£££

£££

Directions: The site is situated on the A9 just north of Dunbeath, the site entrance is 50 metres up the road to Houstry.

Directions: On the A830 Fort William-Mallaig road. Turn left onto B8008 at Arisaig. Signed on left in approximately one mile.

GPS: N58°15.025'W003°25.267'
OS grid: 11 ND 166 299

GPS: N56°55.638'W005°51.552'
OS grid: 40 NM 652 883

All Year

Easter - October

SCOTLAND

John O'Groats Caravan and Camping Site [36]

John O'Groats, Caithness, Highlands,
KW1 4YR Tel: 01955 611329
www.johnogroatscampsite.co.uk

Right in the heart of the action but once pitched on the well kept grass you can relax and enjoy panoramic views of the Pentland Firth, one of the most dangerous shipping channels in the world with spectacular tidal races. You can also see the Island of Stroma, the Orkney Islands and Duncansby Head Lighthouse. Grey Seals are often seen swimming close to the beach.

| NA | 4 | | NP | 90 | | 16 AMP | |

Pub adjacent. Shop ¹/₂ mile. Slipway John O'Groats. RV's 2.

£££   🐕   ††   M   ⓘ   WiFi

Directions: Situated at the end of the A99.

GPS: N58°38.613'W003°04.115'
OS grid: 7 ND 383 731

April - September

Killegruer Caravan Site [71]

Woodend, Glenbarr, Tarbert,
Argyll, PA29 6XB
Tel: 01583 421241

© Anne Littleson

The site is mostly occupied with static caravans but there are 20 touring pitches right next to and almost on the beach. This is a nice and comfortable tidy site isolated right on the west coast of the Kintyre Peninsula. The beach is sandy interspersed with rocks but body boarding should be possible. The site is within reasonable driving distance of Campbeltown.

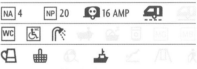

| NA | 4 | | NP | 20 | | 16 AMP | |

Pub 1 mile. Shop ¹/₂ mile. Slipway 5 miles Tayinloan.

£££   🐕   ††   M   ⓘ   WiFi

Directions: Turn right off the A83 one mile South of Glenbarr village. Campbeltown is 12 miles.

GPS: N55°33.363'W005°42.418'
OS grid: 68 NR 663 352

April - October

Lido Caravan Park [17]

South Road, Peterhead, Aberdeenshire,
AB42 2YP Tel: 01779 473358
www.aberdeenshire.gov.uk/caravanparks

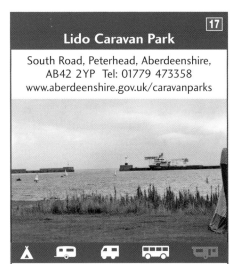

This is a very good local authority site. The sea views are interesting, overlooking Peterhead harbour with its storage tank installations to occupy the mind. Sailing and windsurfing are popular in the safe bay. The site is extremely well cared for with plenty of benches and tables for picnics. Being right next to its own little soft sandy beach and close to the town and the lido where there is plenty to do.

| NA | 4 | NP | 26 | 10 AMP | |

Slipway adjacent.

£££

Directions: In Peterhead on the seafront by the lido.

GPS: N57°29.790'W001°47.842'
OS grid: 30 NK 123 453

March - October

Miltonhaven Seaside Caravan Park [15]

St. Cyrus, by Montrose, Angus,
DD10 0DL Tel: 01674 850413
www.miltonhaven.co.uk

The Park covers six flat and grassy acres bordered by two streams. The 15 touring pitches are close to the seashore and most have a sea view. Miltonhaven has its own sandy, safe swimming beach, with rock pools, adjacent. Bingo on Saturday is a great evening's entertainment. The Coastal Footpath runs directly in front, allowing leisurely walks to the nearby fishing village of Johnshaven.

| NA | 6 | NP | 15 | 10 AMP | |

Dogs allowed but not with tents.

£££

Directions: Two miles North of St. Cyrus. At the crossroads of the A92 and the B9120 turn South East towards the sea. The site is on the right in about half a mile.

GPS: N56°46.830'W002°22.377'
OS grid: 45 NO 775 655

April - September

SCOTLAND

7 Monturpie

Upper Largo, Near St Andrews,
Fife, Scotland, KY8 5QS
Tel: 01333 360254 www.monturpie.co.uk

On the top of a hill, Monturpie Guest House is a traditional stone built farmhouse, both the campsite and house have terrific views overlooking the Firth of Forth towards Edinburgh and Leith. This adult only campsite is superb and is beautifully cared for with newly built toilets and showers. 15 minutes walk downhill takes you to a wonderful little village shop. There is a coffee shop and licensed restaurant, open Thursday to Sunday on site.

| NA 5 | NP 24 | 10 AMP | | |

Pub and shop 1/4 mile at Upper Largo.

£££

Directions: From the South, A915 to Upper Largo to St Andrews Road, the site entrance is on the right just past the end of the village.

GPS: N56°13.288'W002°55.203'
OS grid: 59 NO 433 039

March - October

70 Muasdale Holiday Park

Muasdale, Tarbert, Argyll, PA29 6XD
Tel: 01583 421207
www.muasdaleholidays.com

© Alison Clements

A two acre site split in two with statics on one side and tourers and tents the other. Right beside the beach with beautiful views of the islands. Pitches are narrow and tents over 12 feet will require two pitches. You can jump from your pitch onto the soft white sand. An ideal location if you are looking for peace and tranquillity, convenient for ferries to Arran, Gigha, Islay and Jura.

| NA 2 | NP 15 | 10 AMP | | |

Pub 4 miles. Shop in village 100 metres. Slipway Tayinloan.

£££

Directions: Follow Glasgow M8 signposted Erskine Bridge, cross bridge and pick up the A82 towards Crianlarich and Loch Lomond, continue to Tarbert and pick up the A83 towards Campbeltown, continue through Inveraray, Lochgilphead and Tarbet (Loch Fyne). Muasdale is 22 miles South of Tarbert and 15 miles North of Campbeltown.

GPS: N55°35.873'W005°41.148'
OS grid: 68 NR 678 399

Easter - Mid October

Mossyard Caravan Park

Gatehouse of Fleet, Castle Douglas, Dumfries and Galloway, DG7 2ET
Tel: 01557 840226 www.mossyard.co.uk

This is a 6¹/₂ acre, mostly level, nicely mown site with most pitches having a view of the sea. Indeed some are very close to the rocky and sandy shore. The site is part of the working farm where the McConchie Family have welcomed campers for three generations. It is a beautiful place and exceptionally well maintained with large open grass areas giving a great feeling of space.

Directions: Three quarters of a mile off the A75 West of Gatehouse of Fleet.

NA 6¹/₂   NP 36   10 AMP

Shop 1 mile. Showers 20p.

GPS: N54°50.433'W004°15.625'
OS grid: 83 NX 550 516

March - October

SCOTLAND

Muldaddie Farm House CL [81]

Port Logan, Stranraer, Dumfries & Galloway, DG9 9NJ Tel: 01776 860212
www.caravanclub.co.uk

This is a slightly sloping site on a cliff edge overlooking the Bay and Port Logan. It is a very clean and tidy site with good access and beautiful panoramic views across the Bay. Port Logan is only a short walk away with its little harbour and pub.

| NA 2 | NP 5 | 16 AMP | | |

| WC | | | | | MG | MB |

Pub, shop and beach 1/2 mile.

£££   M   WiFi

Directions: Follow North Stranraer road on A77. Within 1 3/4 miles continue onto the A716 signposted Drummore. In about 10 miles turn right onto the B7065 signposted Port Logan. Site is through village just past village hall.

GPS: N54°43.277'W004°57.700'
OS grid: 82 NX 093 403

Easter - October

North Ledaig [66]
Caravan Club Site

Connel, Oban, Argyll, PA37 1RU
Tel: 01631 710291
www.caravanclub.co.uk

© Tony Hardley.

This 30 acre park is situated on a two mile sand and shingle beach on Ardmucknish Bay where sailing, water sports and safe bathing can be enjoyed. Some of the pitches are almost at the water's edge and all pitches face the sea and enjoy a panoramic view to the beautiful Isle of Mull. The site is ideal for children and has a new adventure playground adjacent to the site.

| NA 30 | NP 280 | 10 AMP | | |

| WC | | | | | MG | MB |

Pub 1 mile.

£££   M   WiFi

Directions: From Oban on the A85. In Connel turn right onto the A828 signposted Fort William at the crossroads of Connel Bridge taking you under a bridge with a clearance of 13 1/2 feet. You will find the site on the left in about one mile.

GPS: N56°28.660'W005°23.935'
OS grid: 49 NM 907 368

Easter - October

Northern Lights [49]

Croft 9, Badcaul, Dundonnell,
Ross-shire, IV23 2QY
Tel: 07786 274175

This wonderful little six acre site is kept neat and tidy and well mown. There is room for 12 touring caravans, motorhomes or tents with some hard standings. The facilities are housed in a sympathetically refurbished old stone building. Access to sandy beaches is about four miles. Being surrounded by hills TV reception is very poor, but makes for a dramatic sea and landscape.

| NA | 6 | NP | 12 | 10 AMP | | |

| WC | | | | | | |

Pub 4 miles. Shop 1/2 mile. Showers 50p.

£££

Directions: From Inverness follow the signs to Ullapool and take the A835 until you come to Braemore Junction. Follow the signs Wester-Ross Coastal Trail A832. Follow the road for approximately 19 miles. You will pass the Dundonnell Hotel on your left. The site is four miles past hotel on your right.

GPS: N57°52.060'W005°20.078'
OS grid: 19 NH 024 914

April - September

Oban Caravan and [67] Camping park

Gallanachmore Farm, Gallanch Road, Oban.
Argyll, PA34 4QH Tel: 01631 562425
www.obancaravanpark.com

Superb for all campers the nine acre site is part of a working farm, set alongside the coast road and overlooking the Sound of Kerrera. This is a very interesting and attractive mainly level site with some hard standings and very helpful staff. There are beautiful views all round and it is a very nice place to visit with masses to do. Nestled in great walking country the sea is within easy walking distance.

| NA | 9 | NP | 150 | | | |

| WC | | | | | | |

Pub and Shops 2 1/2 miles.

£££

Directions: From Oban town centre follow the signposts Gallanach. The site is 2 1/2 miles along the coast road.

GPS: N56°23.395'W005°31.010'
OS grid: 49 NM 830 272

April - September

SCOTLAND

Portnadoran Caravan Site 60

Arisaig, Inverness-shire,
PH39 4NT
Tel: 01687 450267

© Audrey MacDonald

The site is right on the edge of a soft white sandy beach interspersed with rocks. There are stunning views as the site overlooks the islands of Skye, Eigg, Rhum and Muck. It is a wonderful informally managed commercial site that people return to year after year. Porpoises and otters are seen locally and kids will love the rock pooling. Small boats can be launched from site.

NA	4	NP	40	10 AMP		
WC					MG	

Pub 1/2 mile. Shop 2 miles. Fridge/Freezer for use of campers. Showers 20p.

££

Directions: On the A830 Fort William-Mallag road, turn left onto B8008 at Arisaig. Signed on the left in approx two miles.

GPS: N56°55.977'W005°51.643'
OS grid: 40 NM 650 891

April - October

Riverview Caravan Park 13

Marine Drive, Monifieth, Dundee,
DD5 4NN Tel: 01382 535471
www.riverview.co.uk

This is a beautifully maintained 51/2 acre level site. 45 hard standing, serviced pitches are available most having a view of the sea over hedges. Impeccably clean toilets and showers, indeed the whole site is well looked after also offering a sauna, steam baths and gym. Just over a fence there is an enormous expanse of golden beach on the tidal River Tay.

NA	51/2	NP	45	10 AMP		
WC					MG	

Pub and Shop 5 minutes walk.

£££

Directions: From Dundee on the A930 in Monifieth take the next turning on the right past Tescos, (Reform Street). At the end of the road turn left and then take the next road on the right under the bridge (height 10ft 6in), site then signed on the left.

AA ►►►► Scottish TOURIST BOARD ★★★★★ HOLIDAY PARK

GPS: N56°28.768'W002°48.767'
OS grid: 54 NO 502 321

All Year

Point Sands Holiday Park

Tayinloan, Argyll, PA29 6XG
Tel: 01583 441263 www.pointsands.co.uk

A level site right on the sea where you can pitch directly next to the soft sandy beach. There are absolutely superb views over the bay to the Isles of Gigha, Islay, and Jura. Ideal for families, the children's play area is unfenced in the camping field. The long sandy beach offers safe bathing, sailing, windsurfing and other water sports.

NA 16	NP 80	16 AMP		
WC				MG	MB

Pub 1 mile. Showers 50p.

Directions: 17 miles South of Tarbert on the A83 Campbeltown Road. The site is one mile down a drive and on the seashore.

GPS: N55°40.320'W005°38.960'
OS grid: 62 NR 698 484

April - October

Rosemarkie Camping and Caravanning Club Site 32

Ness Road East, Rosemarkie, Fortrose, Ross-shire, IV10 8SE
Tel: 01381 621117 www.siteseeker.co.uk

⬕ 🚐 🚙 🚌 🚎 £££ 🐕 👫 Ⓜ ⓘ WiFi

On the shore of a half-moon bay this is a very attractive level site. There are absolutely beautiful views looking over the Moray and Cromarty Firths. This spectacular coastline is famous for its bottlenose dolphins, which are seen most days from the site. The Fortrose & Rosemarkie golf course is next door. You can walk a short way into a very interesting little town and there is a regular bus service to Inverness.

Directions: The A832 to Fortrose taking the turning right by the Police Station, down Ness Road and first left into a small turning at a Golf Club sign.

NA 6	NP 60	☠ 16 AMP	🚐	🚐
WC	♿	🚿	🛁	📷	🗑	MG	MB

🔌 🏪 🔍 ⛴ ✏ 🏔 🏃

Pub and Shop 10 minute walk.

GPS: N57°34.997'W004°06.537'
OS grid: 27 NH 739 569

March - October

Sandend Caravan Park

23

Sandend, Portsoy, Banffshire, AB45 2UA
Tel: 01261 842660

| Å | 🚐 | 🚍 | 🚌 | 🚎 | £££ | 🐕 | ♀♂ | M | ⓘ | WiFi |

Set in a conservation village and overlooking the gorgeous flat, golden, sandy beach of Sandend Bay with sea access from the site. Everything is neat, tidy and the site is level. Many of the pitches have wonderful sea views. Body boarding will amuse children for hours and a short walk takes you to Findlater castle.

NA 4½	NP 48	💬 10 AMP	🚐	🚐
WC	♿	☔	🚰	♨	⚫	MG	MB
📶	⛲	🔍	⚓			

Pub 1 mile. Showers 20p.

Directions: Three miles West of Portsoy, turn North off the A98 road to Sandend. The site is on the right in half a mile adjacent to an old school and a sandy beach.

GPS: N57°40.930'W002°44.947'
OS grid: 29 NJ 555 661

April - October

SCOTLAND

Sandyhills Bay Leisure Park

Sandyhills, Dalbeattie, Dumfries & Galloway, DG5 4NY
Tel: 01387 780257 www.gillespie-leisure.co.uk

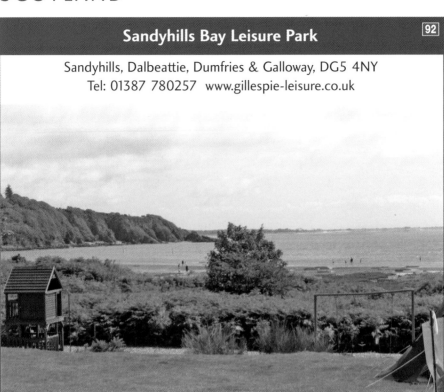

🏕 🚐 🚙 🚌 🚐 £££ 🐕 ♀♂ M (i) WiFi

Professionally maintained, this is a really attractive site. Ideal for families and also having useful shop and good facilities. Directly accessible from site, the long sandy beach has a good tidal range and there is even some salt marsh. The bay provides safe swimming and the wooded hill provides a harmonious backdrop to the site. The area is dotted with smugglers' coves which are accessible at low tide.

Directions: Take the A710 coast road from Dalbeattie to Dumfries. The site is on the right at Sandyhills village just past the golf course.

| NA | 4 | NP | 54 | 🚽 16 AMP | 🚐 | 🚐 |

| WC | | | | | | |

🚰 🛒 🔍 ⛴ ⚓ 🎢 🏃
Pub and Shop 5 minutes.

GPS: N54°52.795'W003°43.852'
OS grid: 84 NX 890 549

April - October

Sango Sands Caravan & Camping Site

44

Durness, Sutherland, Highlands, IV27 4PP
Tel: 01971 511726

A large sprawling site which allows you to find little nooks and crannies to pitch on. You can even park on the cliff edge with a near sheer drop to the sea below. The ground is partly level and partly sloping. The sandy bay is edged by rocky cliffs and the nearby islands make this ideal for snorkelling and body boarding. The beaches are a one minute walk away.

Directions: On the A838 in Durness village overlooking Sango Bay.

NA 10	NP 104	16 AMP

Shop 200 metres.

GPS: N58°34.108'W004°44.603'
OS grid: 09 NC 405 678

April - October

Sauchope Links Caravan Park [12]

The Links, Crail, Fife, KY10 3XL
Tel: 01333 450460
www.largoleisure.co.uk

Beautifully maintained with impeccable facilities, the site is mostly level although parts are sloping. There are static caravans and 50 touring pitches some with hard standings, but all with good views, with the front row having an uninterrupted outlook across the rocky shoreline. Within walking distance is the charming town of Crail, with its steep narrow streets, harbour and sandy beach.

| NA 20 | NP 50 | 10 AMP | | |

Pub 1/2 mile.

£££

Directions: Turn right off the Crail/Balcomie road one mile North East of Crail.

Scottish
TOURIST BOARD
★★★★★
TOURING
PARK

GPS: N56°15.697'W002°36.793'
OS grid: 59 NO 624 080

Easter - October

Seaview Camping and Caravan Park [65]

Kielcroft, Benderloch, Oban,
Argyll, PA37 1QS
Tel: 01631 720360

This is a pleasant site with reasonably level field and some hard standings. It is a lovely quiet peaceful place with views of the bay and hills across the fields. The beach is a short walk away and the site is handy for Forest walks and Tralee Rally Carting. Fresh water charges may apply.

| NA 4 | NP 40 | 16 AMP | | |

Pub 2 miles. Shop 1/2 mile.

£££

Directions: Turn right off the A85 Oban/Connell road onto the A828 and cross Connell bridge signposted Fort William. In three miles just past Benderloch village turn left into the road signposted South Shian/Tralee. The site is on the left in about 500 yards.

GPS: N56°29.780'W005°24.648'
OS grid: 49 NM 901 387

April - September

August 09 ✓

Scourie Caravan & Camping Park   45

Harbour Road, Lairg, Sutherland, Highlands, IV27 4TG
Tel: 01971 502060 (No bookings taken)

A four acre site with a good view of the bay. The 60 pitches are on level ground with some on hard standings. The site has excellent facilities, is well laid out, very tidy and close to the shops and beach. The water is exceptionally clear making it ideal for skin diving. Golden eagles, deer, otters, badgers, wildcat and pine martins can be seen in the nearby hill walking country. Seals can also be seen locally. No advanced bookings are taken for this site, just turn up.

Directions: On the A894 in Scourie overlooking Scourie Bay 26 miles from Durness and 45 miles from Ullapool.

| NA | 4 | NP | 65 | 5-13 AMP | | |

Slipway 200 metres.

GPS: N58°21.088'W005°09.313'
OS grid: 09 NC 154 446

April - September

SCOTLAND

August 09. ✓

Shieldaig Camping Area

Shieldaig Village, Ross-shire, IV54 8XW

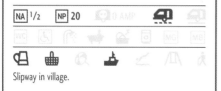

This is a village grazing area where camping is permitted. This is a beautiful spot and the exceptional environment should be well respected. There are superb views over Lochs Shieldaig and Torridon often with beautiful sunsets. Being unsupervised and unserviced except for a water tap, campers are trusted to donate about £5 in the honesty box.

| NA 1/2 | NP 20 | 0 AMP | | |

Slipway in village.

£££

Directions: The site is situated in Shieldaig village off the A896 between Lochcarron and Kinlochewe. From the south leave the A896 at the second sign for the village, site on the left in 400 metres.

GPS: N57°31.530'W005°38.878'
OS grid: 24 NG 816 542

April - October

Shore Caravan Site

106 Achmelvich, Lochinver, Sutherland, Highlands, IV27 4JB
Tel: 01571 844393

An attractive site with plenty of space, pitches are part level, part sloping with some hard standings. If you want a sea view you must make sure that a sea view pitch is available when you book. The seascape almost looks Mediterranean and the silver sand in the bay and flotilla of small craft all add to the ambience.

| NA 6 | NP 60 | 16 AMP | | |

Slipway 4 1/2 miles at Lochinver.

£££

Directions: On the A837 half a mile before Lochinver turn right onto the B869 signposted Stoer, Drumbeg, Achmelvich. In 1 1/2 miles turn left signposted Achmelvich for 1 1/2 miles. In the village go past telephone box straight onto site about 250 yards at the end of the road.

GPS: N58°10.138'W005°18.427'
OS grid: 15 NC 055 248

April - October

Silversands Caravan Site — 58

Portnaluchaig, Inverness,
PH39 4NT
Tel: 01687 450269

Nicely mown and level, this is a lovely little site but the facilities are basic. Pitches are distributed in little nooks and crannies all over the place providing seclusion for those who want it. Access to the sea is only a very short walk and there is good rock pooling. Campers really love this site despite the facilities and it can be very busy at weekends.

NA		NP 18	0 AMP		
WC					

Pub 2 miles. Shop 2¹/₂ miles.

££

Directions: On the A830 Fort William-Mallag road, turn left onto B8008 at Arisaig. Site on left in 2¹/₂ miles next to the Caravan Club CL.

GPS: N56°56.362'W005°51.480'
OS grid: 40 NM 653 898

March - October

Tantallon Caravan and Camping Park — 4

North Berwick, East Lothian, EH39 5NJ
Tel: 01620 893348
www.meadowhead.co.uk/tantallon

Overlooking the Firth of Forth from an elevated position the site is right next to the Glen Golf Course and the beach. A truly magnificent level site spread across several acres with static caravans on one side and masses of room for tourers, most with electric hook-ups, all with a glorious view of the sea and the fascinating small islands. Beach access is down a footpath.

NA 10		NP 140	10 AMP		
WC				MG	MB

Pub 750 metres. Shop 5 minute walk to Tesco.

£££

Directions: The site is situated on the A198 Dunbar - North Berwick road one mile past Tantallon Castle.

GPS: N56°03.338'W002°41.433'
OS grid: 67 NT 571 848

March - October

SCOTLAND

The Croft [57]

"Back of Keppoch" Arisaig, Inverness-shire,
PH39 4NS
Tel: 01687 450200

This is a slightly sloping site with basic facilities. It is however in a wonderful part of the world in an interesting sandy and rocky bay. The views are very beautiful and being west facing there could be spectacular sunsets. There is direct access to the sandy beach and its rocky outcrops and rock pools.

| NA 3 | NP 17 | 10 AMP | | |

| WC | | | | | MG | MB |

Pub ¹/₂ mile. Shop 1¹/₂ miles.

£££

Directions: On the A830 Fort William-Mallag road, turn left onto B8008 at Arisaig. Turn left at 'Back of Keppoch' and follow road for approximately half a mile and site entrance signed on right.

GPS: N56°55.398'W005°51.548'
OS grid: 40 NM 647 881

Easter - October

Thorntonloch Caravan Park [1]

Innerwick, Dunbar, East Lothian,
EH42 1QS
Tel: 01368 840236

Right on its own beautiful surfing beach this site mostly accommodates static caravans. Ten touring pitches are set aside all with hard standings, a standpipe close by and electric hook-up. The toilet blocks and whole site is immaculately kept. There are beautiful views of the coastline and it is adjacent to a soft sandy beach with surfers providing visual entertainment.

| NA 1¹/₂ | NP 10 | 6 AMP | | |

| WC | | | | | MG | MB |

Pub 7 miles. Shop 3 miles. Small boats from beach.

£££

Directions: Seven miles south of Dunbar on A1 signed Thorntonloch, site in 400 metres.

GPS: N55°57.778'W002°23.988'
OS grid: 67 NT 751 745

March - October

Traigh CL

Tigh-Na-Bruaich, Arisaig, PH39 4NT
Tel: 01687 450645
www.traighgolf.co.uk

Everyone gets a beautiful sea view from this slightly sloping Caravan Club CL The beach is only a few metres away. This CL is immediately next door to Silversands campsite.

Pub 2 miles. Shop 2^1/$_2$ miles Arisaig.

Directions: On the A830 Fort William-Mallag road, turn left onto B8008 at Arisaig. Site on left in 2^1/$_2$ miles.

GPS: N56°56.362'W005°51.480'
OS grid: 40 NM 654 898

All Year

West Murkle CL

1 West Murkle, Thurso, Caithness, Highlands, KW14 8YT Tel: 01847 896405
www.westmurkle.co.uk

Nestling in between Thurso Bay and Dunnet Bay lies Murkle where this wonderful little Caravan Club CL is located. Only two pitches enjoy sea views. The beach is a mixture of sand and pebbles which is two hundred yards down an easy to walk path. This is great place for a few days tranquillity away from the hustle and bustle of this modern world.

Pub and Shop 2 minutes at Castledown.

Directions: Turn right off the A9 at Thurso onto the A836 signposted Castletown. After 2^3/$_4$ miles turn left signposted West Murkle. Within one mile at a T-junction turn right. After half a mile turn right through a gate onto a gravel road across a field to a second cattle grid gate and the site is on your left.

GPS: N58°36.403'W003°26'425'
OS grid: 12 ND 165 693

All Year

SCOTLAND

Aberlady Station Caravan Park `5`
Haddington Rd, Longniddry, East Lothian, EH32 0PZ
Tel: 01875 870666
From Haddington take the A6137 for about 4¹/₂miles
to Aberlady. The site is on the left quite close to the
village and close to the sea.

Argyll Caravan Park `74`
Inverary, Argyll PA32 8XT
Tel: 01499 302285
www.argyllcaravanpark.com
The site is on the A83 two miles South of Inverary

Balkenna `77`
Girvan Road, Turnberry, Ayrshire KA26 9LN
Tel: 01655 331692
www.balkenna.co.uk
Four miles North of Girvan. Half a mile South of
Turnberry.

Bayview Caravan Site `43`
Talmine by Lairg, Sutherland, Highlands. IV27 4YS
Tel: 01847 601225
From the A836 through Tongue across Causeway and
turn right onto the Melness Road to Talmine and follow
the signpost to the site.

Burghead Beach Caravan Park `29`
Burghead, Elgin, Morayshire. IV30 2UN
Tel: 01343 830084
www.lossiemouthcaravans.co.uk/burghead.asp
The site is in Burghead off the B9013 road. Eight miles
North West of Elgin adjacent to a sandy beach.

Burrowhead Holiday Village `87`
Isle of Whithorn, Newton Stewart, Dumfries & Galloway,
Scotland, DG8 8JB
Tel: 01988 500252
www.burrowheadholidayvillage.co.uk/
Two miles South West of the Isle of Whithorn 24 miles
South West of Newton Stewart.

Castle Bay Caravan Park `79`
Portpatrick, Stranraer, DG9 9AA
Tel: 01776 810462
From the South take the A75 from Dumfries. Entering

Portpatrick take the first left hand turn past the war
memorial. Continue for three quarters of of a mile
going under an old railway bridge and in 50 yards you
will reach the site entrance.

Craig Tara Holiday Park `75`
Bourne Leisure, Donure Road, Ayr. KA7 4LB
Tel: 01292 265141
If you are coming from the North take the A77 towards
Stranraer. Second right after Bankfield roundabout
South of Ayr. From Doonholm road take a left at the
junction and immediate right into Greenfield Avenue.
At the next junction go left and follow signs for Heads
of Ayr.

Craigdhu Camping & Caravan Site `42`
Bettyhill, Sutherland, KW14 7SP
Tel: 01641 521273
On the A836 Tongue/Thurso Road in the village of
Bettyhill.

Dornoch Caravan & Camping Park `33`
The Links, Dornoch, Sutherland,
Tel: 01862 810 423
www.dornochcaravans.co.uk
From Tain on the A9 road, North, for seven miles and
then turn East onto the A949 for two miles. Turn right
at the bottom of the town square onto Church Street
and River Street.

Fiunary Camping and Caravan Park CS `68`
Morven, Argyll, PA34 5XX
Tel: 01967 421225
After crossing Corran/Ardgour car ferry. Take A884 to
Lochaline, turn right on to B849 for 4¹/₂ miles, site on
left.

Greenpark Caravan Site `34`
Brora, Sutherland, KW9 6LP
Tel: 01408 621513
www.greenparkcaravans.co.uk
On the A9 road 1¹/₂ miles North of Brora. The site is
on the right and is signposted.

Halladale Inn Caravan Park `41`
Melvich, Sutherland, KW14 7YJ

SCOTLAND

Tel: 01641 531282
www.halladaleinn.co.uk
From Thurso on the A836 to Tongue. When you get to
Melvich the site is well marked.

Knock School Caravan Park   `86`
Monreith, Newton Stewart, Wigtownshire, DG8 8NJ
Tel: 01988 700414
www.knockschool.com
Located on the A747, three miles South of Port William
and seven miles North of the historic town of Whithorn.

Leven Beach Holiday Park   `9`
North Promenade, Leven, Fife. KY8 4HY
Tel: 01333 426008
www.pettycur.co.uk/holiday-park2/
Find the North end of Leven promenade and follow
signs for the caravan site.

Lossiemouth Bay Caravan Site   `28`
East Beach, Lossiemouth, Moray, Scotland, IV31 6NW
Tel: 01343 813980
www.lossiemouthcaravans.co.uk
Off the A941 road five miles North of Elgin. The site is
signposted and you turn right down Church Street and
follow signs for Seatown and the caravan site.

Maryport Caravan Site   `82`
Mull of Galloway, Drummore , Stranraer, DG9 9RD
Tel: 01776 840 359
South on the A716 to Drummore. Follow the sign to
Maryport. The site is right at the end of the road.

New England Bay Caravan Club Site   `83`
Port Logan, Stranraer, DG9 9NX
Tel: 01776 860275
www.caravanclub.co.uk
From the East on the A75 and about two miles past
Glenluce fork left onto the B7084, signposted
Drummore. In about six miles continue onto the A716
signposted Drummore. The site is on the left in about
six miles about one mile past the B7065 junction.

Peninver Sands Caravan Park   `72`
Peninver, Cambeltown, Argyll. PA28 6QP
Tel: 01586 552262

www.peninver-sands.com/
From Campbeltown take the B842 road. Just before
Peninver the site is on the right.

Pettycur Bay Caravan Park   `8`
Pettycur Bay Holiday Park, Burntisland Road, Kinghorn,
Fife, Scotland, KY3 9YE
Tel: 01592 892200
www.pettycur.co.uk
Half a mile West of Kinghorn on the A921. The site is
well signed.

Portsoy Caravan Park   `25`
The Links, Portsoy, Aberdeenshire, AB45 2RQ
Tel: 01261 842695
In Portsoy turn North off the A98 to Church Street. In
120 yards turn right into Institute Street. The Caravan
Park is on a sheltered bay overlooking the Moray Firth.

Queensberry Bay Holiday Park   `93`
Powfoot, Annan, Dumfriesshire DG12 5PN,
Tel: 01461 700205
www.queensberrybay.co.uk

Resipole Caravan Park   `62`
by Acharacle, Argyll, Argyllshire. PH36 4HX
Tel: 01967 431235
www.resipole.co.uk
West on the A861 Corran to Salen road. The site is on
the right eight miles West of Strontian.

Rosehearty Caravan Park   `20`
Aberdeenshire Council, Shore Street, Rosehearty,
Fraserburgh, Aberdeenshire, AB43 7JQ
Tel: 01346 571658
On the seafront in Rosehearty overlooking the beach.

Sands Holiday Centre   `53`
Gairloch, Wester Ross, Ross-shire, Highlands, IV21 2DL
Tel: 01445 712152
www.highlandcaravancamping.co.uk
Follow the A832 to Gairloch. At Gairloch take the
B8021 to Melvaig. A four mile drive will bring you to
the holiday centre.

SCOTLAND

Sands of Luce Holiday Park `84`
Sandhead, Stranraer, Wigtownshire. DG9 9JN
Tel: 01766 830296
www.sandsofluceholidaypark.co.uk
From the A75 three miles West of Glenluce turn South
onto the A716 towards Drummore. The Holiday Park is
on the left approaching Sandhead.

Seaward Caravan Park `90`
Kirkcudbright, Dumfries & Galloway DG6 4TJ
Tel: 01557 331079
www.gillespie-leisure.co.uk
Take the A755 from Kirkcudbright for half a mile and
then turn South onto the B727 towards Borgue. The
site is on the right in two miles.

Seton Sands Holiday Village `6`
Longniddry, East Lothian. EH32 0QF
Tel: 01875 813333
www.british-hoildays.co.uk
Takes the A1 as far as the Tranent slip road. Turn onto
the B6371 for Cockenzie and then turn right onto the
B1348. The site is well signposted and is one mile along
on the right.

Shell Bay Caravan Park `11`
Elie, Fife. KY9 1MB
Tel: 01333 330283
1 1/2 miles North-West of Elie then turn off the A917
and follow the road to Shell Bay. This is a single track
road but there are passing places. The site is well
signed.

Station Caravan Park `30`
West Beach, Hopeman, Moray. IV30 5RU
Tel: 01343 830880
In Hopeman off the B9012 road near the harbour.

Strathlene Caravan Site `27`
Great Eastern Road, Strathlene, Buckie, Moray.
AB56 1SR
Tel: 01542 834851
www.ukparks.co.uk/strathlenecaravan
On the Coastal Trail between Cullen and Buckie. Follow
the tourist board signs for Strathlene Caravan Park.
From the A98 Cullen to Fochaber Road take the A942
Coastal Trail. The caravan site is located at Port Essie
between a golf course and Buckie.

Stroma View Caravan & Camping Park `37`
Stroma View, Huna, John O' Groats, Wick, Caithness,
Highlands. KW1 4YL
01955 611313

Follow the A99 road to John O'Groats and turn left at
the Sea View Hotel. Follow the A836 Thurso Road for
one and a half miles. The site is on the left opposite the
island of Stroma.

Tayview Holiday Park `14`
Monifieth, Dundee. DD5 4NN
Tel: 01382 532837
www.tayview.info
In Monifieth turn South off the A930 road signposted
'Caravan Site'. Turn left at the T-junction then first
right under the railway bridge with a height restriction
of 10ft 3in. After 150 yards turn right along the
esplanade for 300 yards.

The Esplanade Caravan Park `18`
Harbour Road, Fraserburgh, Aberdeenshire, Grampian.
AB43 9TB
Tel: 01346 510041
www.aberdeenshire.gov.uk/caravanparks/locations/
fraserburgh.asp
Off the A90 road half a mile from Fraserburgh town
centre overlooking a beach.

Thurso Caravan & Camping Park `40`
Scrabster Road, Thurso, Sutherland, Highlands.
KW14 7JY
Tel: 01847 805500
In Thurso adjacent to the A836.

Thurston Manor Holiday Home Park `3`
Innerwick, Dunbar. EH42 1SA
01386 840643
Two miles South of Dunbar on the A1 signposted for
Innerwick and Crowhill.

Wairds Park Beech Road Caravan Site `16`
Johnshaven, Montrose, Tayside. DD10 0EP
Tel: 01561 362395
On the A92 road nine miles North of Montrose. Turn
right at the Johnshaven signpost. Follow the road to the
harbour turning left onto the beach road. Turn right at

the T-junction and the site is on your left at the end of the road.

West Barr Farm Caravan Park 85

Port William, Wigtownshire, Dumfries and Galloway. DG8 9QS
Tel: 01988 700367
Two miles North-West of Port William on the A747.

Wester Bonnyton Farm 19

Gamrie, Banff, Grampian. AB45 3EP
Tel: 01261 832470
On the Banff Fraserburgh Coastal Trail B9031 two miles East of MacDuff.

Woodland Gardens Caravan & Camping Site 10

Blindwell Road, Lundin Links, by Leven, Fife. KY8 5QG
Tel: 01333 360319
www.woodland-gardens.co.uk
Turn North of the A915 Kirkcaldy - Leven - St Andrews Road at the East end of Lundin Links.

Footpath Cullen Bay, Moray

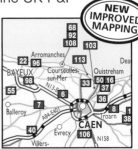

Abermawr, Pembrokeshire

St Brides Bay, Pembrokeshire

WALES

Ramsey Sound, Pembrokeshire

Campfire Cooking

Caerfai Bay, Pembrokeshire

Freshwater, Pembrokeshire

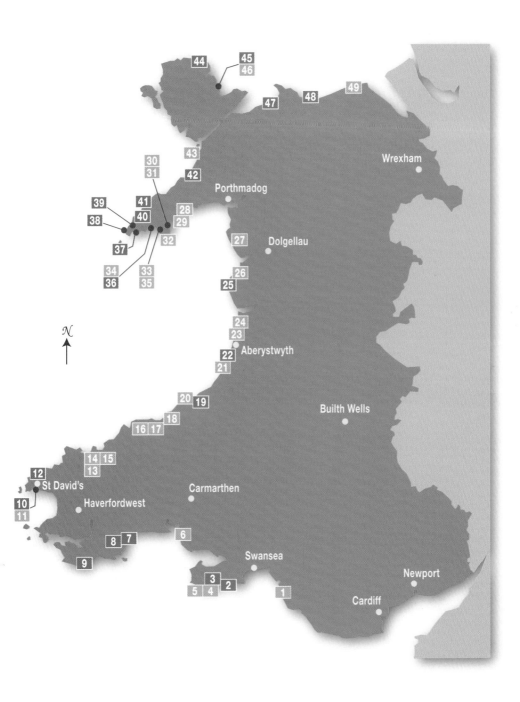

WALES

WALES

Aberafon Camping and Caravan Site

42

Gyrn Goch, Caernarfon, Gwynedd, LL54 5PN
Tel: 01286 660295 www.aberafon.co.uk

Being beautifully located, this site has pitches in a sheltered valley, some on a large field adjacent to and overlooking the sea and some almost on its own private bathing beach. The surroundings are altogether delightful, with panoramic views and seascape, creating a peaceful relaxing atmosphere but is ideal for children to play and explore. The site is at the foot of the 1,500ft Gyrn Goch mountain. There is good river fishing nearby also excellent mountain and coastal walks.

Directions: From Caernarfon take the A487 south to Llanwnda, at the roundabout bare right onto the A499. Go through the village of Clynnog-Fawr then in about one mile at Gyrn Goch turn right at the red shed into a narrow lane. The campsite is at the end of the lane. Warning, the lane is very narrow and not suitable for large vans.

NA 10   NP 65   10 AMP

WC

Shop and pub 1 mile at Clynnog-fawr. Slipway on site.

GPS: N53°00.548'W004°23.166'
OS grid: 123 SH 400 484

March - September

Bron-Y-Wendon Touring Park [48]

Wern Road, Llanddulas, Colwyn Bay,
LL22 8HG Tel: 01492 512903
www.northwales-holidays.co.uk

A very well kept site with the pitches organised in small groups all having beautiful coastal view. The beach is a short walk away. Llanddulas village has shops and pubs. The long Promenade follows the vast sweep from Old Colwyn to Penrhyn Bay giving easy access to the wonderful beaches, pier and harbour at Rhos-on-Sea all joined by a cycle track. Slipways are situated along the promenade for fishing, sailing, and jet skiing.

| NA | 8 | NP | 130 | 16 AMP | | |

| WC | | | | | MG | MB |

Pub, shop and beach 1/4 mile.

£££

Directions: Take the A55 into North Wales, turn off at Junction 25 for Llanddulas then take the first right, back under the A55 and follow the brown tourist signs for the caravan park located on the left.

GPS: N53°17.508'W003°38.763'
OS grid: 116 SH 904 785

All Year

Caerfai Bay Caravan and Tent Park [10]

St David's, Haverfordwest, Pembrokeshire,
SA62 6QT Tel: 01437 720274
www.caerfaibay.co.uk

Popular with families, virtually every pitch has an almost 180° sea view across St Brides Bay. Facilities are excellent and spotlessly clean. The site is right on the Pembrokeshire Coast Path and it is a short walk down to the beach to the beautiful Caerfi Bay. The St. David's Peninsula is an excellent location for anyone who appreciates the beauty of unspoilt coastal scenery and countryside. The amenities of St David's are just a 10 minute walk.

| NA | 9 | NP | 120 | 10 AMP | | |

| WC | | | | | | MG | MB |

Slipway at Porthclais.

£££

Directions: From the A487 Haverfordwest to St David's road turn left just as you enter St David's, signposted Caerfai. Continue down this road until you see the car park right at the end, the site entrance is on the right.

GPS: N51°52.382'W005°15.446'
OS grid: 157 SM 759 244

March - November

Cae-Du Campsite

25

Cae-Du, Rhoslefain, Tywyn, Gwynedd, LL36 9ND
Tel: 01654 711234

This is an idyllic location, perfect to get away from it all but still has good facilities. The site is divided into several areas, some almost on the beach and some at higher levels but all with a fine view across the sea. The site has a very relaxed atmosphere and open fires are allowed. It's a real pleasure to find that on such an informal site, the facilities are quite modern and beautifully kept.

Directions: Take the A493 coast road south from Fairbourne. Drive through Llwyngwril, continue for 2³/₄ miles turning right off the main road at the sharp left hand bend. Go down the steep track and stop at the farm to book in. If coming from the Aberdyfi direction with a motorhome or caravan it is better to go past the site and turn round in the next lay-by. Slightly tight access down a rough track passing under a railway bridge.

| NA | 10 | NP | 65 | | |
| WC | | | | MG | MB |

Shop 4 miles at Bryncrug. Slipway 7 miles at Tywyn.

GPS: N52°37.992'W004°06.971'
OS grid: 124 SH 569 059

Easter - October

Cei Bach Country Club Touring & Tenting Park 19

Parc-Y-Brwcs, Cei Bach, New Quay,
Ceregigion, SA45 9SL Tel: 01545 580237
www.cei-bach.co.uk

This well kept site overlooks Cei Bach Bay, a very attractive sheltered sandy safe bathing beach. Many of the pitches have a sea view and there are numerous attractions nearby. A pathway leads to the beach and a coastal path from Cei Bach to Aberaeron passes over a waterfall on the way.

| NA 3 | NP 60 | 10 AMP | | |
| WC | | | | MG | MB |

Slipway 2 miles at New Quay.

£££

Directions: From the A487 coast road at Llanarth take the B4342, signposted New Quay. After about two miles pass the Schooner Park caravan site, then in 50 yards turn right at the crossroads for Cei Bach, continue down the lane, over a hump back bridge then take a sharp left turn, continue up the hill and at the top take another sharp left turn, signposted for the beach. The site is just around the corner on the left. RVs: Possible.

GPS: N52°12.660'W004°19.886'
OS grid: 146 SN 408 595

1st March - 8th January

Llecyn Llangwnnadl 41

Llecyn Llangwnnadl, Pwllheli,
Gwynedd, LL53 8NT
Tel: 01758 770347

Located on a working farm this is tidy basic family site with a view of the sea over the hedges. Access to the beautiful and isolated Penllech Beach is about half a mile down the footpath opposite the site entrance.

| NA 4 | NP 35 | 6 AMP | | |
| WC | | | | |

Shop 1/4 mile and 3 miles. Slipway 1/4 mile.

£££

Directions: From Pwllheli take the A495 to Morfa Nefyn, then take the B4412 through Edern and Tudweilog to Llangwnnadl. Turn right towards Porth Colman, follow the Porth Colman signs and the site is on the left in about 1 1/4 miles. RVs: Possible.

GPS: N52°52.271'W004°40.816'
OS grid: 123 SH 194 342

Easter - October

WALES

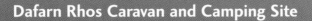

Dafarn Rhos Caravan and Camping Site `45`

Lligwy Beach, Moelfre, Isle of Anglesey, LL72 8NN
Tel: 01248 410607   www.dafarnrhos.wanadoo.co.uk

A friendly family site with beautiful views over Lligwy Bay. The site is partly sloping but many pitches are level and the majority have a sea view. The main toilet and shower facilities are in portacabins that were new in 2007 and are immaculately kept. During the summer kayak and cycle hire is available on the beach that is two minutes from site. Sometimes seals and their pups and even dolphins can be seen close to shore. The coast path follows the cliffs both ways. There is also a designated cycle path that goes past the campsite.

Directions: Cross the Britannia Bridge into Anglesey, take the second exit, A5025, marked Benllech/Amlwch. Continue on the A5025, through Benllech, at the roundabout, take the second exit to Moelfre. Continue down the hill and take the first left after a fish & chip shop. Drive out of the village for approx one mile until you come to a crossroads. Turn right (dead end sign), the site in on the left through a gate. Do not rely solely on GPS!

NA 3.1   NP 85   16 AMP

Pub and shop 1 mile at Moelfre. Slipway 200 metres.

GPS: N53°21.419'W004°15.657'
OS grid: 114 SH 499 864

March - October

Morfa Bychan Holiday Park [22]

Llanfarian, Aberystwyth, Ceredigion,
SY23 4QQ Tel: 01970 617254
www.hillandale.co.uk

This well maintained holiday site has good facilities that were rebuilt in 2006. Most touring pitches are sloping but all have a wide view of the sea. The attractive reception/shop stocks basic essentials, manned by friendly and helpful staff. There is direct access to a private pebble beach.

| NA 3 | NP 65 | 10 AMP | | |

Pub 2 miles at Llanfarian. Slipway 5 miles at Aberystwyth.

Directions: The easiest access to the site is from the south. Take the A487 coast road north from Aberaeron. About four miles north of Llanrhystud turn off to the left and follow the tourist signs for about two miles to the site. Access/pitches for RVs: Possible.

GPS: N52°22.354'W004°06.020'
OS grid: 135 SN 157 766

April - September

Morfa Mawr Farm [37]

Morfa Mawr Farm, Aberdaron, Pwllheli,
Gwynedd, LL53 8BD
Tel: 01758 760264

This farm site spreads over two fields, the larger is flat and set aside for tents only, both have a fabulous view over Aberdaron Bay. There is access directly to the beach, which is about a three minute walk down hill. Facilities are a good standard.

| NA 3 | NP 53 | 6 AMP | |

Pub, shop and slipway 2/3 miles at Aberdaron.

Directions: From Aberdaron take the coastal road signposted Rhiw. The site is down the first track on the right, about two thirds of a mile from Aberdaron.

GPS: N52°48.333'W004°41.842'
OS grid: 123 SH 184 263

March - October

Mynydd Mawr Camping and Caravan Site 38

Llanallawen Fawr, Aberdaron, Pwllheli, Gwynedd, LL53 8BY
Tel: 01758 760223 www.aberdaroncaravanandcampingsite.co.uk

Gloriously isolated this informal site has the most wonderful views and a great view to the sea in two directions. Right on the edge of the National Trust protected area there is one flat and one partly sloping field. The facilities, although basic, are clean and well kept, with the unexpected bonus of two 'family bathrooms' complete with shower, toilet and basin. There are good walks in the area and the adjoining headland is a popular attraction for walkers.

Directions: Fork right off the B4413 (Llanbedrog - Aberdaron) about 3¹/₄ miles past Pen-Y-Groeslan. In about one mile take the right turn signposted Uwchmynydd, carry on past the chapel on the right and the site is about one mile on the left, approximately a quarter of a mile past the Ty-Newydd Campsite. A map with directions can be found on the site's website.

NA 1¹/₄   NP 30   6 AMP

WC

Shop 2 miles at Aberdaron.

GPS: N52°47.703'W004°45.353'
OS grid: 123 SH 143 255

March - October

Nicholaston Farm Caravan and Camping Site [3]

Nicholaston Farm, Penmaen, Gower,
SA3 2HL Tel: 01792 371209
www.nicholastonfarm.co.uk

Three fields provide accommodation on this mostly sloping site being part of a working farm. Most pitches on the caravan field have a fine south facing view overlooking the beautiful Oxwich Bay. This sandy beach is always popular with young families. Access to the beach is only a short walk from the site and you can walk a couple of miles along the beach to Oxwich. The showers and toilets are nicely incorporated into the farm buildings. Nicholaston Farm is a family campsite and does not have a bar/clubhouse but does have a Farm Shop, Cafe, and Pick Your Own fruit on site.

| NA | 14 | NP | 120 | 10 AMP | |

| WC | | | | | |

Pub 2 miles at Oxwich.

££

Directions: The site is situated off the A4118 South Gower road from Swansea to Port Eynon. Go through the village of Penmaen, then, just as you enter Nicholaston, the farm is signed on the left. Turn left down the lane and the farm is a few yards on the left. Park in the farmyard, the campsite reception is in the Farm Shop/Cafe.

Cymru Wales
★★★★

GPS: N51°34.477'W004°07.991'
OS grid: 159 SS 523 884

Easter - October

Plasffordd CL [40]

Plasffordd, Aberdaron, Pwllheli. LL53 8LL
Tel: 01758 760439
www.caravanclub.co.uk

A flat site with a distant view of the sea. This site is quiet, secluded and very reasonably priced. Across from the site entrance at the house a toilet and shower are available. Access to the sea is in about one mile at Whistling Sands.

| NA | 3/4 | NP | 5 | 16 AMP | |

| WC | | | | | |

Pub, shop and slipway 1 1/2 miles at Aberdaron.

££

Directions: Fork right off the B4413 at Llanbedrog - Aberdaron. Travel on B4417 towards Aberdaron. Pass Aberdaron boundary sign and fork right by council houses (200 yards past river/bridge) and turn right at cross roads signed for 'Whistling Sands'. Site in one mile.

GPS: N52°49.299'W004°43.728'
OS grid: 123 SH 162 284

April - October

WALES

Rhosson Ganol Farm

St David's, Pembrokeshire,
SA62 6PY
Tel: 01437 720361

Trefalen Farm

Bosherton, Pembroke, Pembrokeshire,
SA71 5DR
Tel: 01646 661643

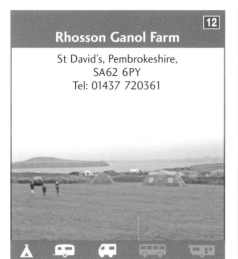

The site is spread over two fields in an idyllic, isolated location with far reaching views across to Ramsey Island. This is an informal site, popular with families returning year after year. The facilities are adjacent to the farmhouse across the road. Whilst not new, they are more than adequate and were newly painted and perfectly clean when we visited.

A beautiful informal site, consisting of two fields. One is mainly flat and used for caravans and motorhomes, the other is partly sloping and is used mainly for tents. The site facilities, although basic, are well kept and clean. A peaceful and remote site only a short distance from the unspoilt sandy beach of Broadhaven. The site is on the 186 mile Pembrokeshire Coast Path and next to the National Trust's Stackpole Estate.

NA	3^1/$_2$	NP	41
WC			

Pub and shop 1^1/$_2$ miles at St David's. Slipway 2 miles at Porthclais.

NA	20	NP	90
WC			

Shop 5 miles. Pub 1 mile. Slipway 3 miles.

£££

£££

Directions: From St David's head west following signs to St Justinians. The site is about 1^1/$_2$ miles from St David's on the left hand side, when entering follow the sign to the Camping & Caravanning Club Certificated site. The owner's farmhouse is on the other side of the road a few metres before the entrance.

Directions: Take the B4319 south from Pembroke and follow signs to Bosherton. In Bosherton pass the church on the left then turn left just past St Govans Country Inn, signed Broad Haven. The site is one mile down the lane just before the car park at the end of the road. Call at the white farmhouse, on the sharp left hand bend, to book in before entering the site.

GPS: N51°52.721'W005°18.287'
OS grid: 157 SM 726 252

GPS: N51°36.443'W004°55.635'
OS grid: 158 SR 974 939

Easter - October

All Year

Three Cliffs Bay Caravan Park

[2]

North Hills Farm, Penmaen, Gower, Swansea, SA3 2HB
Tel: 01792 371218   www.threecliffsbay.com

Excellent facilities and an absolutely superb view from most pitches over Three Cliffs Bay. The Independent in 2006, voted this the Number One View in the Whole World from a Campsite. The site is mostly sloping but some level ground is available. Booking is essential in school holidays. Nearby is Oxwich Bay sandy beach that is always popular with young families.

The site is situated off the A4118 South Gower road from Swansea to Port Eynon. After passing the village of Parkmill turn sharp left just on entering Penmaen. The site is signposted.

Cymru Wales

| NA | 5 | NP | 65 | 8 AMP | | |

Pub 1 mile. Slipway 2 miles at Oxwich Bay.

GPS: N51°34.674'W004°06.969'
OS grid: 159 SS 543 879

April - October

Treheli Farm Campsite 36

Treheli, Rhiw, Pwlheli, Gwynedd, LL53 8AA
Tel: 01758 780281

This is one of those sites people keep returning to, the relaxed atmosphere and fabulous view right across Porth Neigwl (Hells Mouth Bay) makes it a must. The site is on a narrow strip above the bay and the view is uninterrupted. Open fires are allowed on certain parts of the site. The basic facilities are adjacent to the farmhouse where there is also a spring water tap. A steep walk leads down to the beach, a long stretch of sand and stones, exposed to the full force of the Atlantic. Though popular with surfers the beach seldom gets busy. Note that bathing can be dangerous here, with strong undertows and cross currents.

Directions: Take the A449 from Pwllheli to Llanbedrog, at Llanbedrog turn right onto the B4413. Continue on the B4413 through Mynytho, just after the village bare left then after approx three miles turn right. The site is a few hundred yards on the left, opposite the farm. Call at the farmhouse before pitching.

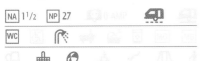

| NA | 1 1/2 | NP | 27 |

Pub 4 miles at Abersoch. Slipway 4 miles at Aberdaron.

GPS: N52°49.541'W004°36.671'
OS grid: 123 SH 242 285

March - October

Trevayne Farm Caravan and Camping Park [7]

Monkstone, Saundersfoot, Pembrokeshire, SA69 9DL Tel: 01834 813402
www.camping-pembrokeshire.co.uk

A popular family site on a working farm. The pitches are spread over several fields so a pitch with a sea view should be stated when booking. Site facilities are very good. There is private access to the beach at Monkstone Bay, a 10 minute walk down a cliff path with steps all the way. Bass and mackerel fishing are especially good at high tide here. At low tide a large sandy beach is created, a lovely alternative to the busier beaches at Saundersfoot and Tenby, which have all the attractions you would expect of popular seaside resorts.

| NA 21 | NP 140 | 10-16 AMP |
| WC | | | | | MG | MB |

Pub 1 mile at New Hedges. Slipway 1 1/2 miles at Saundersfoot. Note: Black water disposal down a manhole.

£££

Directions: Take the A478 south from its junction with the A477, signposted Tenby. At the New Hedges by-pass roundabout turn left onto the B4316, then take the first right into New Hedges, and turn immediately left where you see the campsite sign. The site is in about three quarters of a mile. Access/pitches for RVs: Possible.

GPS: N51°41.788'W004°41.511'
OS grid: 158 SN 141 032

Easter - October

Tyddyn Du Touring Park [47]

Conwy Old Road, Penmaenmawr, LL34 6RE
Tel: 01492 622300
www.tyddyndutouringpark.co.uk

A beautifully kept adults only (over 18) site with panoramic views across Conwy Bay to The Great Orme at Llandudno and over to Anglesey and Puffin Island. Snowdonia National Park is easily accessed with glorious walks for the beginner and enthusiast. An award winning beach is about 15 minutes walk. The camp site has excellent facilities including a well equipped utility/laundry room. The Championship golf course at Conwy is a couple of miles away and Penmaenmawr's delightful course is just 200 metres.

| NA 5 | NP 100 | 16 AMP |
| WC | | | | | MG | MB |

Pub 100 yards. Shop 1/2 mile. Beach 10 minutes. Slipway 1 mile.

£££   WiFi

Directions: Take the A55 west from Conwy for five miles then turn left at the Penmaenmawr roundabout, Junction 16. Turn immediately left and the site entrance is about 300 yards on the right, after The Gladstone pub. Max size 25 feet.

Cymru Wales
★★★★

GPS: N53°16.593'W003°54.369'
OS grid: 115 SH 730 772

March - October

Ty-Newydd Farm Caravan & Camping Site 39

Uwchmynydd, Aberdaron, Gwynedd, LL53 8BY
Tel: 01758 760581 www.tynewyddfarm-site.co.uk

This is a tidy and well cared for site popular with families. The small on-site cafe cooks all day breakfasts and afternoon cream teas. There is a fine view across to Bardsey Island and plenty of good walking in the area. Much of the coast is owned by the National Trust. The adjoining headland is a popular attraction ideal for walks. The surrounding views are delightful with stunning sunsets, panoramic views of mountains and seascape creating a peaceful atmosphere for relaxation.

Directions: Fork right off the B4413 (Llanbedrog - Aberdaron) about 3¹/₄ miles past Pen-Y-Groeslan, in about one mile take the right turn signposted Uwchmynydd, carry on past the chapel on the right and the site is about three quarters of a mile on the left.

NA 5   NP 30   6 AMP

WC

Pub, shop and slipway 2 miles at Aberdaron.

GPS: N52°47.835'W004°45.078'
OS grid: 123 SH 146 257

March - October

Tyddyn Isaf Caravan and Camping Park [44]

Lligwy Bay, Dulas, Angelsey, LL70 9PQ
Tel: 01248 410203
www.tyddynisaf.co.uk

A family run, spacious and well laid out hillside site with excellent security. The touring pitches are on the upper part of the site and most benefit from a fine sea view. There is a large children's play area and the owners have planted thousands of trees & shrubs to create a conservation area and haven for wildlife. The beach at Lligwy Bay is just 250 yards away along the site's own private footpath. Cycle & kayak hire available on the beach in summer.

| NA 22 | NP 42 | 10 AMP | | |

Slipway 2 miles.

£££

Directions: As you enter the Isle of Anglesey on the A5025 over the Britannia Bridge take the second junction, marked Benllech & Amlwych. At the top of the slip road turn right, follow the A5025 through Pentraeth and Benellech then at roundabout turn left. After about a mile, at Brynefail, turn right opposite the telephone box. Follow the signs for Tyddyn Isaf down the narrow lane, the site entrance is in about half a mile on the right.

GPS: N53°21.758'W004°16.535'
OS grid: 114 SH 487 875

Easter - September

Windmills Caravan Park [8]

Narberth Road, Tenby, Pembrokeshire,
SA70 8TJ Tel: 01834 842200
www.windmillscamping.co.uk

A quiet, select site, with beautifully kept, closely mown grass. The facilities, although not new, are well kept and clean. Good sea views over to Tenby & Caldy Island. A footpath at the site entrance takes you three quarters of a mile downhill to North Beach & Tenby. Saundersfoot and Tenby have all the attractions you would expect of popular seaside resorts and offer cafes and restaurants appealing to all tastes and wallets. The 186 mile Pembrokeshire Coast Path runs nearby.

| NA 4 | NP 15 | 10 AMP | | |

Pub 1/2 mile at New Hedges. Slipway 2 miles at Saundersfoot.

£££

Directions: Take the A478 south from its junction with the A477, signposted Tenby. About three quarters of a mile south of the New Hedges roundabout turn left where you see the campsite signboard. The site is about quarter of a mile on the left.

GPS: N51°40.057'W004°42.553'
OS grid: 158 SN 128 019

April - October

WALES

Aeron Coast Caravan Park　20
North Rd, Aberaeron, Ceredigion, SA46 0JF
Tel: 01545 570349
www.aeroncoast.co.uk
On the Northern edge of the Aberaeron main coastal road take the A487. The site is 200 yards from the town centre and harbour.

Bank Farm　4
Horton, SA3 1LL
Tel: 01792 390228
www.bankfarmleisure.co.uk
A4118 pass through Knelston and Scurlage. One mile after Scurlage turn left for Horton at Moor Corner Farm. The entrance is 100 yards on the right.

Beach View Caravan & Camping Park　29
Sarn Beach, LL53 7BZ
Tel: 01758 712956
From Abersoch take the A499 road to Sarn Bach over the crossroads at the top of the hill. Turn left past the Post Office and church then take the left turning signposted, 'Beach View'. The site is on the left in three quarters of a mile.

Blaewwaun Farm　16
Mwnt, Cardigan, Ceredigion, SA43 1QF
Tel: 01239 612165/01239 613456
www.blaenwaunfarm.com
North of Cardigan on the B4548 Gwbent and Mwnt, first right for Mwnt and follow the signs.

Bodafron Caravan Park　46
Bellech, Angelsea, LL74 8RU
Tel: 01248 852417
www.bodafonpark.co.uk
On the Isle of Anglesey half a mile North of Bellech on the A5025.

Bryn Bach Campsite　31
Tyddyn, LL53 7BT
Tel: 01758 712285
www.abersochcamping.co.uk/acc.html
Continue from the A499 in Abersoch. At the signpost in a quarter of a mile turn left to Bwichtocyn. In half a mile continue into a hardcore lane which is rather narrow. The site is in 200 yards.

Caerau Farm　30
Aberdaron, LL53 8BG
Tel: 01758 760481
www.cefnhedog.co.uk
On the B4413 at Pwllheli where you take the A499 to Abersoch. At Llanbedrog turn right and take the B4413 signposted, Aberdaron. Follow the main road through the villages and after Rhoshirwaun you will find Caeraw Farm on the left-hand side on the outskirts of Aberdaron.

Camarthen Bay Touring and Camping Park　6
Tanylan Farm, SA17 5HJ
Tel: 01267 267306
From junction 48 of the M4 follow signs to Pembury Country Park. At Pembury on the A484 follow signs to Kidwelly. Turn at the Spar shop and after 400 yards turn left onto the coastal road. Continue for two miles and the camping park is on the right.

Carreglwyd Camping & Caravan Park　1
The Seafront, Port Eynon, SA1 3LN
Tel: 01792 390795
www.carreglwyd.com
Follow the A4118 from Swansea to Port Eynon a distance of about 18 miles. Carreglwyd is situated adjacent to the village and sandy beach.

Cilan Riding Centre　33
Cilan Fawr, LL53 7DD
Tel: 01758 713276
www.abersochholidays.net
Take the A499 from Pwllheli to Abersoch. From the centre of Abersoch take the road out of the village to Sarn Bach, continue for one mile passing a chapel and telephone kiosk on your right, take the first right turning. Continue down the lane to Cilan Fawr which is on the left at the end of the lane. Ask for Emlyn and Hilda.

Deucoch Touring & Camping Site　35
Sarn Beach, LL53 7LD
Tel: 01758 713293
www.ukparks.co.uk
From Abersoch on the Sarn Bach Road, keep right up the lane and turn left for the site.

Dolgelynen Caravan Park `17`
B4333, Aberporth,Ceredigion SA43 2HL
Tel: 01239 811095
One mile South East of Aberporth on the B4333. One mile North-West on the A487 Aberaeron Cardigan Road.

Fferm-Y-Cim `32`
Abersoch, LL53 7ET
Tel: 01758 712052
Turn left off the A499 Pwllheli Abersoch road. After crossing the bridge across the river follow the one-way system. Turn right signposted Llanengan. Turn sharp left in by the Harbour Hotel. Continue up the hill, turning left into a farm just passed the Cae Du estate.

Greenways Holiday Park `5`
Oxwich, SA3 1LY
Tel: 01792 390220
Leave the M4 at junction 43 onto the A483 for Swansea. From the outskirts of Swansea continue onto the A4067 signposted Mumbles. In about three miles at Black Pill turn right signposted Bishopstone South, Gower, Port Eynon. In about 3 1/2 miles at Penard Church turn right half a mile to a T-junction where you turn left on to the A4118. Carry on for a mile past Nicholaston signposted 'Nature Reserve' and Oxwich. Enter a two mile long drive, narrow in places and rather steep.

Gwaun Vale Holiday Touring Park `13`
Llanchaer, SA65 9TA
Tel: 01348 874698
www.gwaunvale.co.uk
Roundabout where the A40 Haverfordwest road meets the A487 road to Cardigan. Take the road marked 'Gwaun Valley' and the Gwaun Vale Holiday Touring Park is in about 1 1/2 miles.

Hendre Hall `26`
Llwyngwril, LL37 2JF
Tel: 01341 250322
On the A493 Dolgellau-Tywyn Road opposite the petrol station in Llwyngwril.

Llety Caravan Park `18`
Tresaith, Ceredigion, SA43 2ED
Tel: 01239 810354

www.ukparks.co.uk/llety
From Aberystwyth on the A487 to Cardigan turn right onto the B4333 to Aberporth and take the next turning right signposted, Tresaith. The Llety Caravan Park is on the left in about a mile.

Morawelon Camping and Caravan Site `14`
Parog, Newport, SA42 0RW
Tel: 01239 820565
In Newport. From the A487 turn right at Parog Beach signposted to the end of Parog Road.

Nant Mill Touring Caravan & Tent Park `49`
Nant Mill Farm, Gronant Road, Prestatyn, Denbighshire, LL19 9LY
Tel: 01745 852360
On the A548 half a mile East of Prestatyn near the junction of the A548 and A4574. The site is four miles East of Rhyl.

Ocean View Holiday Park `23`
Clarach Bay, SY23 3DL
Tel: 01970 828425
www.oceanviewholidays.com
Exit the M6 at junction 34, follow signs to Lancaster. Take the A589 to Morecambe then on to Heysham following the signs for Ocean Edge.

Pengarreg Caravan Park `21`
Llanrhystud, Aberystwyth, Ceredigion, SY23 5DH
Tel: 01974 202247
www.utowcaravans.co.uk/pengarreg.htm
Nine miles South of Aberystwyth and just off the A487 in the village of Llanrhystyd opposite a service station.

Pen-Y-Craig Farm Caravan Park `24`
Borth, SY24 5NR
Tel: 01970 871717
Take the A487 three miles North of Abery to Bow Street. Turn left onto the B4353 at Rhydypennav through Landre for about four miles. At Borth turn left at the lifeboat station and continue up the hill on the Clarach Road. At the top of the hill turn right and go down a lane for about 200 yards and turn right at the T-Junction down the country lane to the site.

WALES

Rhos-Y-Cribed `11`
St David's, SA62 6RR
Tel: 01437 720336
One mile South West of St. David's on the road to
Porthclais Harbour.

Sarn Farm `28`
Sarn Bach, Abersoch, LL53 5RG
Tel: 01758 712144
www.lokalink.co.uk/sarnfaen-farm/homepage.htm
On the A499 to Abersoch road and continue South to
Sarn Bach, the site is at the first farm on the left in Sarn
Bach.

Seaview/Trem-Y-Mor Caravan & Camping Park `34`
Sarn Beach, LL53 7ET
Tel: 07967 050170
www.tggroup.co.uk/holidays/seaview.htm
Take the A499 from Pwllheil to Abersoch, following
signs to Sarn Bach through Abersoch. After
approximately one mile take the left turn at the
crossroads. The site is 250 yards along the lane on the
right-hand side

St Ives Touring Caravan Site `43`
Lon-Y-Wig, LL54 5EG
Tel: 01286 660347
www.stivestouringcaravanpark.co.uk
Take the A487 from Caernarfon for approximately three
miles then take the A499 to Pwllheli for five miles to
Pontllyfni and take the first turning right.

Trawsdir Touring Caravan & Camping Site `27`
Llanaber, Barmouth, Gwynedd, LL42 1RR
Tel: 01341 280999
Cardigan Bay 2 1/2 miles North of Barmouth on the
A496 Harlech Road. 7 1/2 miles from Harlech Castle.

Tycaol Farm `15`
Newport, SA42 0ST
Tel: 01239 820264
www.barmouthholidays.co.uk/trawsdir.cfm
500 yards North West of the A487. One mile West of
Newport.

Caerfai Bay Campsite © *Gill Sadler*

Europa Park

PUBLIC FOOTPATH
www.somerset.gov.uk

WEST SOMERSET
COAST PATH

BROADSANDS BEACH

150m THEN 220 STEPS

PZ 741

INDEX

INDEX

INDEX

WALES

CAMPSITE SUBMISSION FORM

Please use this form to update the site information in this guide. We particularly need good photographs that represent the site and where possible show the sea view. Nominations for new sites are very welcome. If site is already listed, complete only sections where changes apply. Please fill in answers in capital letters and circle appropriate symbols.

Site Name:

Address:

Postcode:

Tel. No:

Website:

Units accepted by campsite *Please circle 1 or more symbols as appropriate*

⋏ Tent   🚐 Touring caravan   🚐 Motorhome

🚌 Large vehicles   🚎 Holiday accommodation for hire

Description of site:

NA Number of acres: **NP** Number of pitches:

⚡ Electricity available and amperage:

Symbols, facilities *Please circle as appropriate*

🅿 Level pitches   🅿 All season/ hard standing pitches   **WC** Toilets   ♿ Disabled toilets

🚿 Showers   🛁 Family bathroom   🔲 Laundry   🧼 Dishwashing facilities

MG Motorhome grey water disposal   **MB** Motorhome toilet waste disposal

Symbols, amenities *Please circle as appropriate*

🍺 Pub/bar   🏬 Shop   🏖 Beach   ⛴ Slipway

🎠 Children's play area   🚶 Footpath   🏊 Swimming pool indoor or outdoor

Please see overleaf

CAMPSITE SUBMISSION FORM

Please circle as appropriate

Cost based on two people, one caravan or motorhome with electric in August. Guide prices only.

£	Up to £10 per night	**££**	£10-17 per night
£££	£17-35 per night	**££££**	£35 plus per night

🐾	Dogs allowed onsite	†† Adults (Over 18) only	**M** Members only
CS	Certified Site	**CL** Certified Location	
ⓘ	Internet available	WiFi WiFi Available	

Directions to site:

....

....

....

....

Awards: Tourist Board and AA etc. *See page 12 for more information.*

....

OS grid references – 1:50,000

....

GPS Coordinates in the following format: N49°14.988' W000°16.838'

....

Opening and closing dates:

Photo(s) included: ☐ None   ☐ Emailed   ☐ Photo(s) posted with form

email pictures to: gomotorhoming@hotmail.co.uk

Name and email or address - so information can be credited:

....

....

Please use a separate form for each campsite. Send completed forms to:

Vicarious books, 62 Tontine Street, Folkestone, Kent, CT20 1JP

ask@vicariousbooks.co.uk

Thank you very much for your time.

By supplying details and photographs you are giving unrestricted publication and reproduction rights to Vicarious Books LLP.

CAMPSITE SUBMISSION FORM

Please use this form to update the site information in this guide. We particularly need good photographs that represent the site and where possible show the sea view. Nominations for new sites are very welcome. If site is already listed, complete only sections where changes apply. Please fill in answers in capital letters and circle appropriate symbols.

Site Name:

Address:

Postcode:

Tel. No:

Website:

Units accepted by campsite *Please circle 1 or more symbols as appropriate*

▲ Tent 🚐 Touring caravan 🚐 Motorhome

🚌 Large vehicles 🚐 Holiday accommodation for hire

Description of site:

NA Number of acres: NP Number of pitches:

🔌 Electricity available and amperage:

Symbols, facilities *Please circle as appropriate*

🚐 Level pitches 🚐 All season/ hard standing pitches ␣WC Toilets ♿ Disabled toilets

🚿 Showers 🛁 Family bathroom ☐ Laundry 🍴 Dishwashing facilities

MG Motorhome grey water disposal MB Motorhome toilet waste disposal

Symbols, amenities *Please circle as appropriate*

🍺 Pub/bar 🏬 Shop 🔍 Beach ⚓ Slipway

🛝 Children's play area 🚶 Footpath 🏊 Swimming pool indoor or outdoor

Please see overleaf

CAMPSITE SUBMISSION FORM

Please circle as appropriate

Cost based on two people, one caravan or motorhome with electric in August. Guide prices only.

£   Up to £10 per night   ££   £10-17 per night

£££   £17-35 per night   ££££   £35 plus per night

🐕   Dogs allowed onsite   ††   Adults (Over 18) only   **M**   Members only

CS   Certified Site   CL   Certified Location

ⓘ   Internet available   WiFi   WiFi Available

Directions to site:

....

....

....

....

Awards: Tourist Board and AA etc. *See page 12 for more information.*

....

OS grid references – 1:50,000

....

GPS Coordinates in the following format: N49°14.988' W000°16.838'

....

Opening and closing dates:

Photo(s) included: ☐ None   ☐ Emailed   ☐ Photo(s) posted with form

email pictures to: gomotorhoming@hotmail.co.uk

Name and email or address - so information can be credited:

....

....

Please use a separate form for each campsite. Send completed forms to:

Vicarious books, 62 Tontine Street, Folkestone, Kent, CT20 1JP

ask@vicariousbooks.co.uk

Thank you very much for your time.

By supplying details and photographs you are giving unrestricted publication and reproduction rights to Vicarious Books LLP.

CAMPSITE SUBMISSION FORM

Please use this form to update the site information in this guide. We particularly need good photographs that represent the site and where possible show the sea view. Nominations for new sites are very welcome. If site is already listed, complete only sections where changes apply. Please fill in answers in capital letters and circle appropriate symbols.

Site Name:

Address:

Postcode:

Tel. No:

Website:

Units accepted by campsite *Please circle 1 or more symbols as appropriate*

⚊ Tent   Touring caravan   Motorhome

Large vehicles   Holiday accommodation for hire

Description of site:

NA Number of acres: **NP** Number of pitches:

Electricity available and amperage:

Symbols, facilities *Please circle as appropriate*

Level pitches   All season/ hard standing pitches   **WC** Toilets   Disabled toilets

Showers   Family bathroom   Laundry   Dishwashing facilities

MG Motorhome grey water disposal   **MB** Motorhome toilet waste disposal

Symbols, amenities *Please circle as appropriate*

Pub/bar   Shop   Beach   Slipway

Children's play area   Footpath   Swimming pool indoor or outdoor

Please see overleaf

CAMPSITE SUBMISSION FORM

Please circle as appropriate

Cost based on two people, one caravan or motorhome with electric in August. Guide prices only.

£   Up to £10 per night   ££   £10-17 per night

£££   £17-35 per night   ££££   £35 plus per night

🐕   Dogs allowed onsite   👫   Adults (Over 18) only   M   Members only

CS   Certified Site   CL   Certified Location

ⓘ   Internet available   WiFi   WiFi Available

Directions to site:

Awards: Tourist Board and AA etc. *See page 12 for more information.*

OS grid references – 1:50,000

GPS Coordinates in the following format: N49°14.988' W000°16.838'

Opening and closing dates:

Photo(s) included: ☐ None   ☐ Emailed   ☐ Photo(s) posted with form

email pictures to: gomotorhoming@hotmail.co.uk

Name and email or address - so information can be credited:

Please use a separate form for each campsite. Send completed forms to:
Vicarious books, 62 Tontine Street, Folkestone, Kent, CT20 1JP
ask@vicariousbooks.co.uk

Thank you very much for your time.

By supplying details and photographs you are giving unrestricted publication and reproduction rights to Vicarious Books LLP.

CAMPSITE SUBMISSION FORM

Please use this form to update the site information in this guide. We particularly need good photographs that represent the site and where possible show the sea view. Nominations for new sites are very welcome. If site is already listed, complete only sections where changes apply. Please fill in answers in capital letters and circle appropriate symbols.

Site Name:

Address:

Postcode:

Tel. No:

Website:

Units accepted by campsite *Please circle 1 or more symbols as appropriate*

Tent   Touring caravan   Motorhome

Large vehicles   Holiday accommodation for hire

Description of site:

NA Number of acres: **NP** Number of pitches:

Electricity available and amperage:

Symbols, facilities *Please circle as appropriate*

Level pitches   All season/ hard standing pitches   **WC** Toilets   Disabled toilets

Showers   Family bathroom   Laundry   Dishwashing facilities

MG Motorhome grey water disposal   **MB** Motorhome toilet waste disposal

Symbols, amenities *Please circle as appropriate*

Pub/bar   Shop   Beach   Slipway

Children's play area   Footpath   Swimming pool indoor or outdoor

Please see overleaf

CAMPSITE SUBMISSION FORM

Please circle as appropriate

Cost based on two people, one caravan or motorhome with electric in August. Guide prices only.

£   Up to £10 per night   **££**   £10-17 per night

£££ £17-35 per night   **££££** £35 plus per night

🐕   Dogs allowed onsite   👫   Adults (Over 18) only   **Ⓜ**   Members only

CS   Certified Site   **CL**   Certified Location

ⓘ   Internet available |WiFi| WiFi Available

Directions to site:

Awards: Tourist Board and AA etc. *See page 12 for more information.*

OS grid references – 1:50,000

GPS Coordinates in the following format: N49°14.988' W000°16.838'

Opening and closing dates:

Photo(s) included: ☐ None   ☐ Emailed   ☐ Photo(s) posted with form

email pictures to: gomotorhoming@hotmail.co.uk

Name and email or address - so information can be credited:

Please use a separate form for each campsite. Send completed forms to:
Vicarious books, 62 Tontine Street, Folkestone, Kent, CT20 1JP
ask@vicariousbooks.co.uk

Thank you very much for your time.

By supplying details and photographs you are giving unrestricted publication and reproduction rights to Vicarious Books LLP.

CAMPSITE SUBMISSION FORM

Please use this form to update the site information in this guide. We particularly need good photographs that represent the site and where possible show the sea view. Nominations for new sites are very welcome. If site is already listed, complete only sections where changes apply. Please fill in answers in capital letters and circle appropriate symbols.

Site Name:

Address:

Postcode:

Tel. No:

Website:

Units accepted by campsite *Please circle 1 or more symbols as appropriate*

Ⓐ Tent   🚐 Touring caravan   🚐 Motorhome

🚌 Large vehicles   🚐 Holiday accommodation for hire

Description of site:

NA Number of acres: NP Number of pitches:

💀 Electricity available and amperage:

Symbols, facilities *Please circle as appropriate*

🚐 Level pitches   🚐 All season/ hard standing pitches   WC Toilets   ♿ Disabled toilets

🚿 Showers   🛁 Family bathroom   ⊡ Laundry   🧼 Dishwashing facilities

MG Motorhome grey water disposal   MB Motorhome toilet waste disposal

Symbols, amenities *Please circle as appropriate*

🍺 Pub/bar   🏪 Shop   🏖 Beach   ⚓ Slipway

🎠 Children's play area   🚶 Footpath   🏊 Swimming pool indoor or outdoor

Please see overleaf

CAMPSITE SUBMISSION FORM

Please circle as appropriate

Cost based on two people, one caravan or motorhome with electric in August. Guide prices only.

£	Up to £10 per night	**££**	£10-17 per night
£££	£17-35 per night	**££££**	£35 plus per night

🐕	Dogs allowed onsite	♦♦	Adults (Over 18) only	**M**	Members only
CS	Certified Site	CL	Certified Location		
(i)	Internet available	WiFi	WiFi Available		

Directions to site:

Awards: Tourist Board and AA etc. *See page 12 for more information.*

OS grid references – 1:50,000

GPS Coordinates in the following format: N49°14.988' W000°16.838'

Opening and closing dates:

Photo(s) included: ☐ None   ☐ Emailed   ☐ Photo(s) posted with form

email pictures to: gomotorhoming@hotmail.co.uk

Name and email or address - so information can be credited:

Please use a separate form for each campsite. Send completed forms to:
Vicarious books, 62 Tontine Street, Folkestone, Kent, CT20 1JP
ask@vicariousbooks.co.uk

Thank you very much for your time.

By supplying details and photographs you are giving unrestricted publication and reproduction rights to Vicarious Books LLP.